THIS BOOK IS A GIFT

From: _____

To: _____

Date: _____

WHAT THE BIBLE

actually SAYS

ABOUT MONEY

—31 MEDITATIONS—

SCOTT MORTON
MAPS CREATED BY KATIE MOUM

PRAISE FOR WHAT THE BIBLE *actually* SAYS ABOUT MONEY

Warning! This book may challenge how you think about money. In his conversational style, Scott Morton takes us into the Word for insights and practical principles. Thank you, Scott, for daring us to make financial stewardship a part of our daily walk with the Lord.

– Dave Blomberg
Director of Ministry Partnership
Mission Aviation Fellowship

What the Bible Actually Says about Money biblically addresses the serious challenges we face daily in Africa. When a minister of the gospel raises the topic of money, *congregants hold their pockets with both hands!* This comes from unbalanced teaching on giving and tithing.

The lifestyle issue is also important. Some veer off into the health and wealth gospel, and others believe that if you are rich, you must be consorting with demons! I look forward to using this book, starting with my family, and then to our wider ministry.

– Chris Amulo, The Navigators
National Director, Kenya

More than any other aspect of discipleship, one's attitudes and actions related to money provide a barometer for spiritual maturity. By going directly to Scripture, Morton cuts through the conflicting values of tradition, the church, and culture to examine Kingdom values.

– Donna Wilson
Senior Fundraising Consultant and Coach,
InterVarsity Christian Fellowship

Scott's devotions are a welcome addition to the conversation on earning and giving. His thoughts are sure to challenge you, but they will drive you closer to the Father's heart. Don't just get a copy for yourself, buy copies to share with your family and faith community. They will thank you.

– Marc A. Pitman, CEO
The Concord Leadership Group
LLC Greenville, South Carolina

I found these quick, easy-to-read meditations to be both scripturally based and practical. It's evident they come from Scott's study of the Scriptures as well as the way he has lived his life. Scott's humor and his reflections are counter-cultural and thought-provoking. I found myself taking more time reflecting than in reading the meditation.

Anyone who reflects on these writings will have a deeper understanding of what the Scriptures say about money. Warning! Be prepared to have your thinking challenged.

– Scott Landon
Executive Pastor of Administration
Wheaton Bible Church, Wheaton, Illinois

What the Bible Actually Says about Money, written in Scott's comfortable, sometimes humorous style was truly a gift to me. Myths about how much to give and where to give have circulated for far too long in the body of Christ.

Attitudes toward lack or abundance of money, fear of the future, and the treatment of others with our money spoke to my heart. Looking at Scripture to get a better view of Jesus and how He treated money was helpful. I need this book! And I will share it with others.

– Judy Wolter
Discipler and Bible-study leader in Michigan

Scott Morton, in bite-sized portions, gently guides us in how to live a life of understanding stewardship. Scott is uniquely qualified to speak to the issue of money and heart. Why? Because he lives out what he writes about. He is authentic, and as a result, his words resonate with those who understand discipleship. Read it, buy copies for your friends, and create a movement of responsible stewardship!

– Lauren Libby
President, TWR International

What the Bible Actually Says about Money winsomely helps followers of Christ discover the joy and freedom of biblical financial stewardship. A motivating devotional—it stimulates the mind, warms the heart, and challenges the will. And it is fun! Scripture is offered for meditation in manageable morsels that are augmented by helpful personal examples—a good book to reread often as we seek to invest our resources wisely in Christ's kingdom.

– Mutua Mahiani
International President, The Navigators

This is classic Scott Morton straight from the wealth of his experience. Punchy, persuasive, and penetrating, *What the Bible Actually Says about Money* will challenge your thinking on money by sharpening your understanding of what the Bible says about it. Reflection on the 31 passages will pay dividends (pun intended).

– Grant Dibden, The Navigators
National Director, Australia

As the years of my own leadership in ministry continue to grow, I see more and more how rare is the gift God has given Scott Morton—to get to the absolute truth of God's call for Christians and money. A must-read for every Christian seeking deeper intimacy with Jesus Christ—and for the leaders who accompany them on the journey.

– Jeremy Rude, Vice President
Catholic Christian Outreach, Canada

WHAT THE BIBLE

actually SAYS

ABOUT MONEY

WHAT THE BIBLE
actually SAYS
ABOUT MONEY

What the Bible Actually Says about Money —31 Meditations—
Copyright © 2019 Scott Morton

First Edition: Year 2019
What the Bible Actually Says about Money —31 Meditations— / Scott Morton
Paperback ISBN: 978-1-946453-60-0
eBook ISBN: 978-1-946453-61-7

DEDICATION

To you who hold this book in your hands and desire to include financial stewardship in your walk with God—well done.

CONTENTS

INTRODUCTION

We have been taught to walk with Christ by faithful pastors, Bible study leaders, and maybe an older Christian friend. But our mentors tread lightly on the topic of money because money is "personal." It is often easier to talk about sex than money.

But silence doesn't help. Many church-goers hear about money only during Stewardship Sunday. And like the Starship Enterprise, they pop out their defensive shields. Sadly, no matter what the pastor preaches, the only message they hear is "give more" or "tithe!"

We hear a different money message from "health and wealth" teachers. They try to use the Scriptures to convince you that "God wants you wealthy!" And if you send a seed gift to their ministry, God will pour out a blessing on you. Hmmm.

Our secular culture does us no favors either. It encourages over-spending, over-borrowing, and instant gratification. Faddish practices are preferred over biblical principles.

But our earliest teachers about money are parents and family—our home environment. We were taught (intentionally or unintentionally) some good money values and some not so good. And they are deeply ingrained.

Let's admit that most of our opinions about money have been learned from our own experiences or secondhand rather than from personal study. For example, when dedicated believers are asked, "How much should a Christian give?" this generation answers, "Ten percent to the local church and offerings to the parachurch." But the next generation answers with honest silence or "Whatever moves you emotionally."

Sadly, what the Bible *actually* says about money is often obscured by traditions, fads, and formulas whose moorings to the Bible are convoluted or wispy or ignored.

Here is your opportunity to listen to the Lord about this emotional subject that weaves in and out of our minds daily. This book is not a diatribe exhorting you to give more. The purpose is to provide you with quiet opportunities to reflect on thirty-one classic Scriptures and draw your own conclusions.

This does not mean you are materialistic. Give yourself permission to take a few minutes for thirty-one days to think first-hand about this unspoken subject. God bless you as you seek Him in these Scriptures.

Scott Morton

DAY 1 – GIVING: HOW MUCH IS ENOUGH?

And He looked up and *saw the rich* putting their gifts into the treasury. And He *saw a poor widow* putting in two small copper coins. And He said, "Truly I say to you, this poor widow *put in more* than all of them; for they all *out of their surplus* put into the offering; but she *out of her poverty* put in *all* that she had to live on."

–Luke 21:1–4

The Widow's Mite, Joao Zeferino da Costa, 1876. Public Domain

I HEARD THIS story as a kid at Sunday School. It didn't make sense to me that Jesus commends the widow for giving her last two pennies—everything she had. As a five-year-old theologian with a nickel of offering money in my pocket, I worried about the poor woman.

Since those early days, I have discovered that many believers puzzle over this passage. Are we to give "all?" Let's look more deeply.

This incident took place in the temple treasury at Jerusalem. Secured in the wall were thirteen collection receptacles shaped like trumpets, wide at the bottom and narrow at the top—making it impossible for a passerby to steal.

And here Jesus was watching. *He looked up and saw* the rich and he *saw* the widow put their gifts into the trumpets. That the widow gave anything is noteworthy. She could have excused herself because of her poverty or because she was a widow. Jesus could have rushed in and stopped her—but He didn't.

Then he said the poor widow *put in more* than the rich. How can that be? If Jesus had taken the trumpets off the wall and poured the coins onto the temple floor, those given by the rich would have out-numbered the widow's two lepta—Israel's smallest coin.

Jesus measures giving by a different standard. The rich gave *out of their surplus*—money not needed for day-to-day living, money they would never miss. The widow gave *out of her poverty*—money needed for day-to-day living. By Jesus' accounting method, she gave more.

Is Jesus commending the woman for giving *all* her assets? How then, could she care for herself (or her children)? The common un-derstanding—that she gave her last penny—seems odd.

Perhaps it happened this way: Leviticus 19:13b says, "The wages of a hired man are not to remain with you all night until morning." Accordingly, Jewish landlords paid their workers on the same day they worked—before nightfall.

Having been paid that day or the previous day, the widow went to the temple and gave out of her daily cash flow—"the living that she had" (margin NASB). She gave not out of excess, but sacri-ficially. Her giving cut into her living.

So how much should a Christian give? Most believers say, "A tithe, ten percent." That is what they have been taught. But think about it. If someone earns $200,000 per year and gives ten percent ($20,000), then he or she must eke out a living on $180,000. Does that capture the spirit of Jesus' words?

Jesus teaches a wider principle. Instead of a percentage, how about this:

Give in such a way that it makes a difference in your lifestyle.

For the desperately poor, ten percent may be too much. For most, ten percent is too little. C. S. Lewis famously said, "I am afraid the only safe rule is to give more than we can spare…If our charities [our giving standards] do not at all pinch or hamper us, I should say they are too small."[1]

So, how much should you give? Put ten percent out of your mind. Give like the widow—cut into your lifestyle to give. Let your giving affect your living.

> **Prayer:** Lord Jesus Christ, like the Father, You *see* my giving just as You saw the poor widow's giving in the temple. I'm glad You are watching. I confess that I feel guilty if I don't tithe, and I feel proud if I do. Help me to give in such a way that it cuts into my lifestyle. Help me learn to give generously and sacrificially. Amen.

---

1   C. S. Lewis, *Mere Christianity* (New York: MacMillan Publishing Company, 1952), 67.

DAY 2 – DO YOU SECRETLY WANT TO BE RICH?

> But those who *want to get rich* fall into temptation and a snare and many foolish and harmful desires which plunge men into ruin and destruction. For the *love of money* is a root of all sorts of evil, and some by *longing for it* have *wandered* away from the faith and pierced themselves with many griefs.
>
> – 1 Timothy 6:9-10

NOWHERE DOES JESUS condemn the rich for being rich. Nor does the Apostle Paul. In our passage today, Paul says the problem is *wanting to be rich*. Not possessing wealth but *longing for it* leads to trouble—big trouble—as we shall see.

We must understand three things about this passage.

1. **It is written to Christians.** The phrase *wandered away from the faith* is the tip-off. A non-believer has no faith to wander from.

   For example, a Christian couple in Denver asked for counseling about their financial situation. They attended church regularly, but neither husband nor wife had permanent jobs. They spent hours entering contest after contest hoping for a windfall. Sometimes they won a bag of groceries or a few dollars from the lottery. One day as they were driving down I-25, the husband suddenly pounded both fists on the steering wheel and shouted, "God! I wish I was rich!"

   At least he was honest. It is ironic that some secular people do not seem to have a greedy bone in their bodies while some dedicated believers constantly long for more. You don't have to be rich to want to be rich.

2. **Money is not the problem.** Verse 10 is perhaps the most misquoted verse in the Bible. Money is <u>not</u> a root of evil—*love of money is a root of evil.*

Love of money is called *mammon* by Jesus—"wealth personified as an object of worship" (Matthew 6:24 margin NASB). When money becomes the driving force in our lives, we are worshiping at the Church of the Almighty Dollar!

"People say that money does not satisfy, but it does satisfy if you want to live on that level. People who are satisfied only with the things that money can buy are in great danger of losing the things that money cannot buy."[2]

Money is merely a tool to help us be and do that for which we were created.

3. **We don't bolt—we wander.** Those who want to get rich don't suddenly bolt from Christ—they wander. Slowly, they withdraw from fellowship with believers; they stop reading the Bible and prayer seems mechanical.

This is more serious than merely skipping church. Paul warns that those who *wander from the faith* will encounter temptation, a snare, foolish and harmful desires, ruin, and destruction, piercing themselves with many griefs.

What seems like a harmless desire (wanting to be rich) ends with ruin and destruction.

The ancient LaBrea tar pits in southern California looked harmless because the sticky tar was covered with plant debris. Saber-toothed tigers were lured toward the pits to attack smaller animals already trapped—easy prey. But the big cats themselves became trapped. We study their bones today in the LaBrea museum in Los Angeles.

---

2   Wiersbe, W, *Bible Exposition Commentary - New Testament* (Victor Books, 1989).

Christians become similarly trapped by the lure of *wanting to get rich*. Does this mean that you should not work toward a higher income? Not at all. If providing for your family or pursuing your God-given calling requires more—go for it. But what is your motive?

A caller to financial guru Dave Ramsay's radio show wanted to buy a fast-food franchise. He had a good income, no debt, and his savings accounts were growing. When Ramsay asked why he wanted to buy a franchise, the caller answered, "To increase my income." Ramsay pressed, "Why? For what larger purpose?"

The caller had no other purpose—becoming wealthy was his only goal.

Billy Graham said, "There is nothing wrong with men possessing riches. The wrong comes when riches possess men."

Prayer: Creator of all, I find it easy to criticize others for wanting money, but I realize I, too, am vulnerable. I don't *think* I long to be rich, but perhaps I am deceiving myself. Please speak to me about my heart's deepest values and tell me if I am *wandering from the faith*. Amen.

DAY 3 – SHOULD CHRISTIAN LEADERS ASK FOR MONEY?

> Do we not have a *right* to eat and drink [at the expense of the Church]? Nevertheless, we did not use this *right*, but we endure all things so that we will *cause no hindrance to the Gospel* of Christ.
>
> –1 Corinthians 9:4 and 12

SOME BELIEVERS LOOK down on mission agencies or churches that *ask*. They say that if Christian leaders truly trusted God, they would not lower themselves to ask for money. It's unspiritual. Stories abound of miraculous last-minute funds arriving when all seemed lost. So leaders are advised, "Don't ask, just pray. God's will done in God's way never lacks God's supply."

"Telling only God" was accidentally popularized in the late 1800s by the legendary orphanage director, George Mueller. Knowing his history helps explain his views on asking.

As a child in Germany, Mueller habitually stole money from his father's desk. Then, as a young man, Mueller checked into hotels wearing expensive clothes, but he ducked out without paying.

But in early adulthood, Mueller became a dedicated Christian and eventually a pastor in England. In those days, churches were financed by renting or selling pews to parishioners. Mueller believed this violated the partiality teaching in James 2—welcoming a rich man but ignoring a poor man. So Mueller placed a chest at the back of his church for free-will gifts and promised his congregation he would say nothing about money.

Similarly, at his orphanages, Mueller never asked for money, but he and his team shared answers to prayer about miraculous financial deliverances—like the day the milk wagon broke down in front of the orphanage the very morning they ran out of milk. Plus, he published reports of orphanage finances. Technically, he didn't *ask*, but he indirectly informed prospective donors that the orphanage had financial needs and gave them a way to respond.

Today, Evangelicals have narrowed Mueller's practice into: "Tell only God." As a result, many mission workers and Christian leaders don't speak about money. Often, feeling a sense of shame, they silently try to copy the faith of George Mueller, hoping money will miraculously roll in.

This "no-ask" method is attractive because it avoids the risk of rejection and appears more spiritual, but the Bible contains several examples of *asking* to advance God's kingdom:

- Moses asked the Israelites to give for the desert tabernacle (Exodus 35:1–9).

- Nehemiah asked King Artaxerxes for timber to build Jerusalem's walls (Nehemiah 2:4–8).

- Elijah asked a Gentile widow for support (1 Kings 17).

- Paul asked the Roman Christians to fund his ministry to Spain (Romans 15:20–24).

- Jesus instructed the Twelve and the Seventy to seek worthy hosts for lodging—twice (Matthew 10:5–15 and Luke 10:1–12).

Some say Jesus Himself never asked, but is that true? He asked to borrow a boat, a donkey, and an upper room, and He asked John to care for His mother. He asked people to deny themselves and come after Him (Luke 9:23).

My friend, is it *asking* that bothers you or is it the pushy fundraising of some gospel ministries?

In our passage today, Paul declares that he and other gospel workers had the *right* to be supported by the Church—by believers. But he does not demand his right *(use this right)* because of relational and moral problems in the Corinthian church. Receiving money from the Corinthians would cause *a hindrance to the gospel*.

It's the same today. Pushy fundraising dishonors Christ and hinders the gospel—speak up when you see that! But your annoyance at being asked does not de-legitimize the right of God's messengers to invite God's people to support God's Kingdom.

Yes, we've heard wonderful stories of last-minute deliverances, but we don't hear stories where time ran out and God did not supply. "God's will done in God's way" usually involves inviting others to join you in accomplishing God's will.

> **Prayer:** Creator of the universe, I confess I have sometimes thought that "asking" is sub-spiritual, and I have judged pastors and missionaries negatively for "lowering themselves" to make appeals. Help me to discern manipulative appeals from genuine appeals. Help me keep my eyes on You as the Source and not to be judgmental. Amen.

DAY 4 – HOW DID JESUS FUND HIS MINISTRY?

The twelve were with Him, and also some women who had been healed of evil spirits and sicknesses: *Mary who was called Magdalene*, from whom seven demons had gone out, and *Joanna* the wife of Chuza, Herod's steward, and *Susanna*, and *many others who were contributing to their support out of their private means.*

–Luke 8:1-3

WHERE DID JESUS get money?

- Lived off savings?
- Worked as a carpenter?
- Underwritten by a wealthy benefactor?
- Miraculously multiplied loaves and fishes?
- None of the above

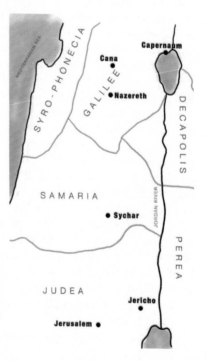

Our text today shows that Jesus was funded by women who had been deeply touched by His ministry—Mary Magdalene, Joanna, Susanna, and *many others who were contribut-*

ing to their support out of their private means.

Simply put, Jesus needed money. For example, while Jesus talked with the woman at the well, "His disciples had gone away into the city [Sychar in Samaria—map] to *buy food*" (John 4:8). His team had a money box—*glossokomen*—originally a small box to house the reed of a woodwind instrument (John 12:6; 13:29). Judas Iscariot was the keeper of it.

This takes the mystery out of how Jesus lived. Of the 2000–3000 meals Jesus ate during His three-year ministry, only three times is it recorded that He miraculously provided food—the feeding of the 4000, the feeding of the 5000, and turning water into wine at Cana (map).

Nor did He (nor His entourage) live off crumbs from the street. Can you imagine Him standing at street corners with a sign saying, "Very hungry. Anything helps"? He was an itinerant preacher—not an itinerant beggar.

Not only these three women, but *many others* gave also. How many? Matthew 27:55–56 names two more besides Magdalene, Joanna and Susanna, and adds, "Many women were there...who had followed Jesus from Galilee while ministering to Him." Mark also records "many other women" (Mark 15:41). Jesus had *many* giving partners.

If Jesus had been a zillionaire or if He had been miraculously financed for three years, how could He understand financial pressure? If He had multiplied loaves and fish for every meal, how could He understand why we clip grocery coupons? He chose to live with the same financial challenges we do—He "gets it."

But if ever a human being did *not* need money, it was Jesus! Could not the One who provided bread and fish for 5000 have funded Himself? Instead, the Son of God held back His miraculous powers and lived in dependence on giving-partners. That's the way the Godhead planned it from the beginning. Amazing!

There's more. In being supported by giving-partners, Jesus established a reproducible model for funding His Kingdom. If He had funded Himself, Magdalene, Joanna, and *many others* would have been denied the honor of partnering in His Kingdom. For 2000 years, giving-partners have supported Christ's worldwide Kingdom from Jerusalem to Irian Jaya to Uzbekistan. Today, you and I have the same honor.

A school teacher was called to serve Christ as a two-year missionary to Russia. Fearful of fundraising, she decided to take money from her savings account—the entire two-year funding amount. But her own mother called her out: "Don't you dare support yourself. Being your financial partner is the only way I will ever get to Russia!"

Giving puts you on the front lines of ministry—along with Magdalene, Joanna and Susanna!

> **Prayer:** God of the cattle on a thousand hills, You could have sent Jesus as independently wealthy without the need for financial support. Thank You for this example of giving and receiving to advance the Kingdom. Forgive me for my selfish desire to be 100 per cent self-sufficient. Help me to see giving and receiving as a privilege rather than an unfortunate have-to. Amen.

DAY 5 – GREED: DO YOU KNOW WHERE YOU ARE VULNERABLE?

> *Beware and be on your guard* against *every form of greed*; for not even when one has an *abundance* does his life consist of his *possessions*.
>
> –Luke 12:15

WE ASSUME THAT today's passage is not meant for us but for greedy people. But greed affects us all, and it sometimes comes in small packages.

Twelve-year-old *Katie* was sharing a basket of cheese fries with her older sister at their hometown hamburger joint. As they were eating, Katie's sister was annoyed. She said, "Katie! Every time I reach for a cheese fry, you grab one just before my hand reaches the basket—even though your mouth is already stuffed."

Years later Katie reflected: I had more cheese fries than I could cram into my mouth, but I wanted more. Why? I don't know. It certainly was not because I was hungry.

In the Greek language, *greed* is *pleonexia*—*pleon*/more; *echo*/to have. *More to have.* It is always used in a bad sense according to Vine's Expository Dictionary. Perhaps you've heard the classic quote from legendary millionaire John D. Rockefeller who was asked, "How much money does it take to be wealthy?" Rockefeller's insightful answer: "Just a little more."

Pleonexia is also defined as covetousness—wanting something that another person has, not because we need it, but because they have it and we don't.

Several phrases in our text need to be highlighted:

1. ***Beware and be on your guard.*** Why would Jesus warn

us to *be on your guard*? Because greed is subtle—we are often not aware when we are greedy. And greed is dangerous—as dangerous as immorality, says the Apostle Paul. "But <u>immorality</u> or any impurity or *greed* must not even be named among you as is proper among saints" (Ephesians 5:3).

Finally, the Ten Commandments don't merely warn about greed—they prohibit it (coveting). "You shall not covet your neighbor's house…your neighbor's wife…*or your neighbor's cheese fries* (Exodus 20:17).

2. ***Every form of greed.*** Greed comes in various forms. A new car or a fancy espresso machine might not tempt you, but you are vulnerable to some *form of greed*— maybe nice clothing or nice restaurants or the latest tech gadget. Let us be careful about criticizing others for their *form of greed*, realizing we, too, have a soft spot. Even if you have walked with Christ for years, you are vulnerable to some *form of greed*.

3. ***Abundance–possessions:*** Finally, Jesus says that *abundance* [of possessions] does not bring abundant living. Many Christians buy into (pun intended) this worldly lie. If you purchase something to boost your self-esteem or to find happiness, it will definitely help—for about 20 minutes.

What about chocolate? Maybe 25 minutes. Sorry.

The third verse of the 1930's hymn "God of Grace and God of Glory" captures our preoccupation with things:

> *"Cure Thy children's warring madness,*
> *Bend our pride to Thy control;*
> *Shame our selfish, wanton gladness,*
> *Rich in things and poor in soul."*

The late author Jerry Bridges coined the term "respectable sins." Overt sins such as stealing, murder, or adultery are condemned by all; they are non-respectable. But coveting is below the surface and seems victimless—a "respectable sin." Nevertheless, it still replaces God with things, which is idolatry, and the victim is you!

My friend, do you know yourself well enough to understand what *form of greed* tempts you?

Prayer: Lord of all, I often consider greed to be problems faced by others, but not me! Today I admit that I, too, am vulnerable. I am tempted to be greedy for _____ and _____. I confess this respectable sin called greed. Help me to seek You first and not be seduced by things. Amen.

DAY 6 – WAS JESUS POOR? WAS JESUS RICH?

> The foxes have holes and the birds of the air have nests, but the Son of Man has *nowhere to lay His head.*
>
> —Luke 9:58

IN THE FUNDRAISING seminars I have taught in many countries, this question generates heated discussions. We want to know how Jesus lived and what that means for us today.

Wanting to be like Jesus, some early church fathers became desert hermits. They owned nothing, had no employment, and spent their days in meditation and sometimes preaching. Poverty was a sign of a close walk with Jesus (so they said). By contrast, throughout church history, many non-hermits considered wealth as a sign of closely following Christ.

But let's examine the evidence. If Jesus was poor, how poor? Or how rich? Here are some clues on both sides.

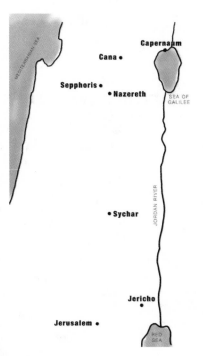

JESUS' PARENTS

- Joseph and Mary presented their baby, Jesus, at the temple with two turtledoves (Luke 2:24). Because they couldn't afford a lamb, doves or pigeons were acceptable (Leviticus 12:8).

- When the Magi visited Joseph and Mary two years later, they came to a "house" in Bethlehem (Matthew 2:11)—not a barn. Had their economic situation improved?

- In Nazareth, Joseph was a carpenter or stone mason (Matthew 13:55). Since Nazareth was only an hour's walk from the Roman resort town of Sepphoris (map), Joseph likely had steady employment in that ever-under-construction city.

JESUS HIMSELF

- Though He didn't have guaranteed lodging each night (our passage today), Jesus doesn't seem to live on the street. In John 1:39, two curious followers "came and saw where [Jesus] was staying…."

- Did Jesus own property? Matthew 4:13 says He "*settled* in Capernaum." The Greek word kataoikeo might imply home ownership. More probably, Jesus *settled* in Peter's mother-in-law's Capernaum home (Mark 1:29 and 35).

- Jesus and the Twelve had a money box (John 12:6 and 13:29). Money for the box was donated by many women who had been touched by Jesus' ministry (Luke 8:1-3).

- Jesus was criticized for *eating and drinking* with sinners (Luke 15:2). Unlike John the Baptist, He didn't live as a desert hermit.

- The Roman soldiers at the crucifixion would not tear Jesus' seamlessly woven robe but cast lots for it—implying it was costly (John 19:23–24).

- Jesus identified with the poor—they gladly came to Him. "Jesus' lifestyle is not of one in a gated community or a corporate office," says Timothy Johnson, a New Testament professor at Emory University in Atlanta. Johnson says that a "rich Jesus" is a distortion of history.

- 2 Corinthians 8:9 states, "Though He was rich, yet for your sake He *became poor*, so that you through His *poverty* might become *rich*." Jesus certainly *became poor* by leaving the multi-faceted riches of the Godhead to dwell as a human on Planet Earth. Through His spiritual poverty (coming to earth and dying for us), we become spiritually rich in Him. This is not a verse about material economics.

JESUS' TEACHING

- Though Jesus never condemned rich people for being rich, He taught that wealth must not become an idol. He told the rich young ruler to sell everything and give to the poor (Matthew 19:16–22). Since His life was consistent with His teaching, Jesus must have lived frugally and generously.

So, was Jesus poor or rich? What is your opinion? And why are we so curious about it?

Prosperity teachers need a rich Jesus to prove that God wants His followers to be rich. Advocates for the poor prefer a poor Jesus. The debate will continue! But instead of forcing a yes or no answer, how about this conclusion:

Jesus secured enough funding to enable Him to accomplish His calling from God.

This is a model we can follow. Let us obtain enough of this world's resources to accomplish the calling God has uniquely given each of us. For some, that requires wealth. For others, not so much.

Now, let's be practical. Would Jesus own a smartphone? If it helped Him accomplish His calling—yes!

My curious friend, what is God's calling to you? How much funding will that require?

> **Prayer:** Lord Jesus, I see that You had enough funding to accomplish the work the Father called You to do. By Your grace, help me to focus on the calling You have put before me. I trust You to enable me to secure enough funding to do what You have called me to do. Amen.

DAY 7 – MONEY, WORRY, AND THE GREAT PROMISE

> *Do not worry* then, saying "What will we eat?" or "What will we drink?" or "What will we wear for clothing?" For the Gentiles eagerly seek *all these things*; for your Heavenly Father knows that you need all *these things*. But seek first His kingdom and His righteousness, and all *these things* will be added to you.
>
> –Matthew 6:31-33

NOTE THE FIRST three words in today's passage: *Do not worry*. Jesus does not say, "*Try not* to worry."

Worry in Greek is *merimna*, and it is used 19 times in the New Testament. It means *to draw in different directions*—to be in two minds, on big things or little things. For example, "I have a promising career, but *what if* I don't get a promotion?" Or "That thumping in my car is probably nothing, but *what if….*?"

Worry's favorite weapon is *what if?*

Worry starts with a legitimate concern but bubbling below the surface like a super-heated geyser is fear. Unchecked, fear morphs into exaggerated what-if's, causing stress. Eventually, health problems can develop—upset stomach, ulcers, irritable bowel syndrome, headache, sleep problems, eczema—and more.

What does worry accomplish? An anonymous quipster said, "Worry is like a rocking chair: it gives you something to do but it doesn't get you anywhere."

But still, we worry. Some say, "I can't stop worrying!" Maybe we can't stop the temptation to worry, but must we collapse into worry every time temptation comes?

In our passage today, Jesus offers two antidotes for worry.

1. **Trust that He knows.** Three times Jesus mentions *these things*—life's necessities—what to eat, what to drink, what to wear. Since our "Heavenly Father knows that you need all these things," we can relax. He is aware of the stuff we worry about.

    If God knows we need *these things*, then like the Psalmist, "We need not fear bad news, nor live in dread of what may happen. For he is settled in his mind that Jehovah will take care of him" (Psalm 112:7 Living Psalms and Proverbs).

    Not only does He know, He cares. 1 Peter 5:7 says, "Casting all your anxiety on Him, because He cares for you."

2. **Believe His promise.** Matthew 6:33 is the Great Promise. To receive *these things* (life's necessities), *seek first His kingdom.* Common sense says you must *seek first* a good job or a good bank account. Focus on your physical needs first and give leftover energy to your spiritual life. But striving for the necessities of life as your #1 priority is no guarantee you will get them. Hard work doesn't guarantee success.

    Instead, seek God's Kingdom first and *all these things will be added to you.* That's a guarantee.

    Does seeking God's kingdom mean we do nothing—waiting in excited holiness for God to bless? Earlier in this same chapter (6:26), speaking about the birds, Jesus said, "Your heavenly Father feeds them; are you not worth much more than they?" But God doesn't drop fresh earthworms into their mouths each morning. When you see a robin poking in the grass, it is looking for the food God has provided. Birds do their part, and God does His part.

But sometimes we worry needlessly. Poet Ralph Waldo Emerson wrote:

Many of your ills you have cured,
And the strongest you have yet survived.
But what torments of grief you endured,
From evils that never arrived.

My friend, are you a worrier? Have you identified the specific fears that lie below the surface of your worries? An honest self-analysis will help.

What would it look like for you to put Jesus and His Kingdom first—before your finances? Are you willing to trust Jesus' Great Promise?

Prayer: Father in Heaven, sometimes I worry about having enough money—but I never considered how my underlying fears might be driving my worry. I want to deliberately seek You first. I trust Your promise that all *these things* will be added to me. Amen.

DAY 8 – WHAT JESUS TAUGHT ABOUT TITHING

> Woe to you, scribes and Pharisees, hypocrites! For you tithe mint and dill and cummin [similar to caraway seeds] and have neglected the weightier provisions of the law: *justice and mercy and faithfulness*; but these are the things you should have done without neglecting the *others*. You blind guides, who strain out a *gnat* and swallow a *camel!*
>
> Matthew 23:23-24

JESUS SPOKE ONLY twice about tithing. First, in Luke 18:11–14, He told of a Pharisee who pridefully thanked God he was better than others—saying, "I fast twice a week; I pay *tithes* on all that I get."

Nearby, a tax collector was praying, "God, be merciful to me, the sinner." Jesus said that the tax collector went home justified rather than the tither. This parable teaches humility—not the practice of tithing (see page 137).

Jesus' second teaching on tithing is our passage today. Jesus does not criticize the Pharisees for *failing* to tithe—they were over-achievers in tithing. The Old Testament called for tithes only on grain, new wine, oil, and firstborn livestock (Deuteronomy 14:23). But the Pharisees tithed on garden plants also. Though meticulous, the Pharisees *neglected* the *weightier provisions of the law: justice, mercy, and faithfulness*. They majored on a minor.

According to Peter Pett's Commentary on the Bible, the Aramaic for gnat is *qamla* and camel is *gamla*—similar sounding words. Jesus' humorous quip about *straining out a gnat* (tiny insect) and *swallowing a camel* (largest animal in Palestine) would have brought laughter to this serious conversation.

So what is Jesus actually saying?

He is speaking to Jewish leaders—followers of the Old Covenant. He said, "These are the things you should have done [justice, mercy, faithfulness] without neglecting the *others*." *Others* is plural—though vague, it likely refers to *other* Old Testament laws. Jesus expects Jews to be good Jews—to follow their historic faith, and that includes tithing.

What about followers of New Covenant? If we bring Old Testament tithing into the New Covenant, must we also bring other Jewish laws—such as dietary rules or circumcision?

Of the 40 times tithing is mentioned in the Bible, 32 are from the Old Testament, including the often-quoted Malachi 3:8–10, "Bring all the tithe into the storehouse."

Some teachers equate "storehouse" with "church-house." But that is a stretch. The storehouse was originally a granary built onto the side of the temple to store excess grain during the reign of Hezekiah 250 years before Malachi.

What about the Apostle Paul? He was a good Pharisee before his conversion—and certainly a tither. Though Paul taught giving to the new churches, he is silent on tithing. Not a peep. His silence cannot be ignored.

Christian leaders are free to exhort you to tithe, but they are not free to insist on tithing as the primary guideline for New Testament giving. That minimizes other New Testament teaching about giving and (though unintended) imposes a "rule" on conscientious believers.

So if tithing is not the guideline, what is? Start your search in the New Testament with Luke 21:1–4 and 2 Corinthians 8–9. If you are looking for a loophole to avoid giving generously to your local church, you will not find it (Galatians 6:10, 1 Timothy 5:17–18).

The New Testament does not mandate a percentage or a formula for giving. You are free! Being free, you will likely give much more than ten percent—and do it joyfully!

Prayer: Father of all, thank You that we are not under the law when it comes to giving. I confess that sometimes I feel I "have to tithe." And sometimes (like the Pharisees) I feel proud about my giving. Help me not to *strain out a gnat and swallow a camel*, and help me not to be judgmental of others' giving. Teach me how to be freely generous. Amen.

DAY 9 – GIVE AND IT WILL BE GIVEN TO YOU—REALLY?

> *Give* and it will be given to you. They will
> *pour into your lap* a good measure—pressed
> down, shaken together and running over.
> For by your standard of measure it will be
> measured to you in return.
>
> –Luke 6:38

GIVE AND IT will be given to you has become a proverb—you're sure to get money back for money given, tit for tat, and more besides. Unfortunately, some preachers have hijacked this verse and made it a formula guaranteeing a financial return for a "seed gift" to their ministry.

Sadly, we are skeptical of this wonderful promise—it seems too materialistic, a guaranteed financial benefit merely for giving a few dollars? But a surprise awaits us as we dive into the context. Look at the powerful verbs starting in verse 28.

6:28 *Bless* those who curse you, *pray* for those who mistreat you.

6:30 *Give* to everyone who asks of you.

6:31 *Treat* others the same way you want them to treat you.

6:35 *Love* your enemies, *do good and lend*, *expecting nothing in return*.

6:36 *Be merciful*.

6:37 *Do not judge*, do not *condemn*, *pardon* and you will be pardoned.

And finally verse 38, *Give*.

Luke 6:28–37 is about building relationships—especially with those who mistreat you. When we love—even unkind people—when we are merciful and uncondemning, when we seek the other person's good, these same people *pour into our lap* even more love, mercy, and non-condemnation than we originally gave. This is the way of discipleship with Jesus as our leader.

They will pour into your lap. The Jews wore a full-length robe that could be pulled up at the waist to form a deep pocket for carrying grain or groceries home from the market.

What about getting money back? Sure, if money is given, money could come back. But notice verse 35—"expecting nothing in return." *Give and it will be given to you* is not a guaranteed formula to manipulate God into blessing you. That is insulting. Jesus' true followers give their hearts in relationships without expecting a return.

The Apostle Paul captured Jesus' teaching in 1 Thessalonians 2:8 when he said to the Thessalonian new believers, "Having so fond an affection for you, we were well-pleased to impart to you not only the gospel of God but also our own lives, because you had become very dear to us."

A missionary was supported with $50 per month for years by a friend in Arizona, but when he lost his job, the support stopped. After a few months, the missionary visited the donor and his wife, spending two nights in their home and treating them to dinners—the missionary paid! They enjoyed two days of mutual encouragement, laughing, reminiscing, prayer, and Bible study.

When the missionary returned home, the Lord prompted him to send the unemployed donor $200—no reason—just because it was needed. The donor wrote back immediately expressing how deeply the $200 had touched him.

A year passed. Finally, the donor found a good job. Soon the couple re-started support of the missionary—not for $50 per month but for $200 per month.

What happened here? The missionary genuinely "gave his heart" to encourage his friends, not to "get something back." But the promise proved true. The $200 per month continues to this day.

My Christian friend, when you give money, do you secretly hope for a financial windfall? Instead, focus on loving and serving others. Let us give our hearts, our emotions, our time, and yes, our money, without expecting anything in return. And see what happens!

To whom can you *give* <u>yourself</u> today?

Prayer: Father in Heaven, I enjoy blessings being poured into my lap, but I hesitate to take the first step to build or rebuild relationships. Help me not to withhold my emotions, my limited time, my limited finances, and my limited energy with people in my world. Help me to be more interested in others than in myself, starting with my own family. Amen.

DAY 10 – EIGHT WAYS TO GO BROKE

THE BOOK OF Proverbs (meaning "sayings" or "comparisons") is not a book of guaranteed promises, but these sayings do predict likely outcomes—things that usually come to pass. And underlying these likely outcomes is a theme: The fear of the Lord.

Here are eight proverbs that predict poverty. To which ones are you most vulnerable?

#1. NEGLIGENCE

> Proverbs 10:4: Poor is he who works with a *negligent* hand, but the hand of the diligent makes rich.

BEING *negligent* IS not the same as being lazy. Negligence is "failure to exercise care." Negligence might be caused by laziness but also by fear or from being naive. If my car runs low on coolant and the engine overheats, I am *negligent*—maybe because I believed my brother when he told me, "The radiator is full."

#2. MERE TALK

> Proverbs 14:23: In all labor there is profit, but *mere talk* leads only to poverty.

A MISSIONARY WAS discouraged and wanted a career change because he struggled with fundraising. A friend begged him to join his multi-level business to make "big money with little work." Providentially, he read this proverb just in time and chose to ignore *mere talk*. As it turned out, his friend made little money.

#3. PROCRASTINATION

> Proverbs 20:4: The *sluggard* does not plow

> after the autumn, so he begs during the
> harvest and has nothing.

IN MID-EASTERN FARMING, plowing and sowing must be done during a short window of time—and it immediately follows the exhausting work of harvest. But that's when the *sluggard* wants to rest. Even if you are tired, do it now!

#4. HURRY

> Proverbs 21:5: The plans of the diligent
> lead surely to advantage, but everyone who
> is *hasty* comes surely to poverty.

THIS SPEAKS TO "get-rich-quick" schemes like lotteries and online gambling. But more subtle is a *hasty* lifestyle. Someone constantly in a hurry makes abrupt decisions and reacts too quickly to the unexpected instead of responding deliberately. That leads to bad financial decisions and, eventually, poverty. Slow down. Make diligent plans.

#5. LOVE PLEASURE

> Proverbs 21:17: He who *loves* pleasure will
> become a poor man; he who *loves* wine and
> oil will not become rich.

THERE'S NOTHING WRONG with pleasure, and there's nothing wrong with oil and wine, but *loving* them brings us to poverty. Proverbs 21:20 says there is "oil and wine in the house of the wise." What's the difference? The wise don't *love* oil and wine.

#6. OVER-DRINKING, OVER-EATING, OVER-SLEEPING

> Proverbs 23:21: For the heavy drinker
> and the glutton will come to poverty, and
> drowsiness will clothe one with *rags*.

GOD MADE US with the wonderful appetites of drinking, eating, and sleeping. But when we drink, eat, or sleep to excess, we are headed for *rags*. Sensual excesses are usually an attempt to escape. What are you running from?

#7. EMPTY PURSUITS

> Proverbs 28:19: He who tills his land will have *plenty* of food, but he who follows empty pursuits will have poverty in *plenty*.

THIS PROVERB HAS a play on words—*Plenty of food or plenty of poverty*. Following idealistic, *empty pursuits*, like once-in-a-lifetime business deals, ends in poverty. If a money-making opportunity is "too good to be true," it is indeed too good to be true.

Is there a specific idealistic pursuit that tempts you? What makes it so attractive?

#8. SEXUAL TEMPTATIONS

> Proverbs 29:3: A man who loves wisdom makes his father glad, but he who *keeps company with harlots* wastes his wealth.

Keeping company with harlots in reality or virtually via pornography costs money—not to mention ruins lives. The prodigal son "devoured [the father's] wealth with prostitutes" (Luke 15:30).

NUMBERS 5, 6, and 8 are related to our appetites and the escapism lying beneath them. Numbers 2, 4, and 7 are similar to visions of grandeur and a dose of reality is needed to escape them. Numbers 1 and 3 have to do with our will—doing what must be done whether we feel like it or not.

My friend, to which of these poverty-producing tendencies are you most vulnerable? Now look below the surface. What makes you vulnerable to these in particular?

> **Prayer:** Father in Heaven, help me to not take the easy way out by giving in to my appetites or feelings. Help me to be a doer and deliver me from delusions of grandeur. Amen.

DAY 11 – JESUS' TWO SURPRISING ECONOMIC VALUES

> Jesus then took the loaves, and having given thanks, He distributed to those who were seated; likewise also of the fish *as much as they wanted*. When they were filled, He said to His disciples, "*Gather up the leftover fragments* so that nothing will be lost."
>
> –John 6:11-12

THIS FAMILIAR PASSAGE reveals two obvious traits about Jesus. But two surprising economic values also pop up—values that fly against today's common sense norms.

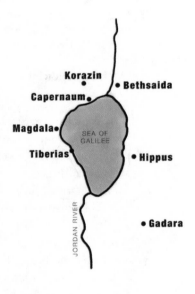

The *Feeding of the 5000* happened at the north end of the Sea of Galilee near Bethsaida. A large crowd followed Jesus to a grassy hill where He was teaching. And now, besides feeding them spiritually, He wants to feed them physically! That's obvious trait #1—Jesus cares about the physical well-being of people—holistic ministry, we say today.

Since Bethsaida was Philip's hometown (John 1:44), Jesus asked him, "Where are we to buy bread so that these may eat?" The disciples had no answer, but they found a boy with five barley loaves and two fish (John 6:9).

You know what happened—Jesus miraculously multiplied bread and fish for 5000. Critics say this was not a miracle but that the crowd was inspired by the boy who shared his loaves and fish. Seeing his generosity, others shared their personal provisions too. Hmmm. But where did the leftovers come from?

Make no mistake—Jesus can do the miraculous. That's obvious trait #2.

Now, for two surprising economic values—Surprise #1 is unexpected generosity. He gave them *as much as they wanted*. If each person had received only one piece of bread and one small dried fish, it still would have been a miracle and the talk of Galilee for years. But Jesus surprised them—*as much as they wanted*—12 baskets of leftovers.

This contradicts the axiom you've been told 100 times, "God supplies our needs but not our wants."

The second economic value: *Gather up* the leftovers. Why? Maybe Jesus didn't want to clutter the grassy field where sheep would graze the next day? Or would the leftovers supply the next day's meal? Or is He simply modeling, "Thou shalt not litter?"

Surprise #2: Though exceedingly generous, Jesus was not wasteful.

Consider the following questions about your own economic values:

1. **Are you unexpectedly generous?** If you tell your waitress that you just came from church, surprise her with a lavish tip. When you see a poor family at Burger King, buy their lunch—including jumbo fries! And for your missionaries, how about a bonus now and then?

   I learned a valuable lesson about unexpected generosity from my wife, Alma. During our university-ministry days, we invited students to our home for Saturday evening meals—including ice cream bars for dessert. Then I would teach a wonderful Bible lesson. The students stayed around—talking, laughing, and praying.

   Finally, a student-leader told me, "Do you know why we like coming here?"

   "Because of the great Bible lessons?" I said humorously.

He replied, "Nope! It's because Alma serves seconds and thirds on ice cream bars—as many as we want."

Unexpected generosity indeed.

2. **Are you wasteful?** During harvest time on the farm, my grandfather caught single kernels of corn in a small bucket as they fell off the elevator. Why let them rot on the ground?

American schools teach the new "Three R's"—re-use, recycle, reduce." Fine, but do you turn off lights in rooms not being used? Do you let your car run, wasting fuel while you sit inside texting? Can you create a meal out of leftovers from the fridge?

At Bethsaida that day, Jesus adhered to the old adage: *Use it up, wear it out; make it do, or do without.*

But thriftiness is not an end in itself. An extreme frugalist might spend hours driving around town searching for bargains but spend wildly on something unnecessary. Frugality can masquerade as spirituality. Extreme frugalists can be as obsessed with money as materialists.

Prayer: Lord of all, help me find ways to be unexpectedly generous to my family, my friends, and to strangers. And show me how to be frugal—not wasting Your resources. I long to be like You. Amen.

DAY 12 – WHERE SHOULD WE GIVE?

A CONSCIENTIOUS YOUNG couple feels obligated to tithe (ten percent) to their local church, but they also want to support a friend doing missionary work in Rwanda. On their tight budget, they can't tithe to their church and significantly support their missionary friend. They are frustrated and ask you for advice.

What would you say?

Four New Testament passages illustrate giving to four groups to advance the gospel—the local church, family, the poor, and missions.

THE LOCAL CHURCH

> Galatians 6:6: The one who is taught the word is to *share all good things* with the one who teaches him.

PAUL INSTRUCTS THE new believers in Galatia (Antioch of Pisidia, Derbe, Lystra, Iconium—map) to *share all good things* with their teachers. Does *sharing all good things* mean merely sharing the spiritual truths they have been taught? No. Galatians 6 is about doing good—especially to the "household of the faith" (6:10). Paul is boldly saying, "Financially support those who teach you!"

In America, studies find that 2 percent of churchgoers give nothing to their church[3], and 34 percent of churchgoers give to four or more organizations [besides their church].[4] Church leaders sadly admit that the Pareto 80/20 principle (law of the vital few) is at work in church giving—80 percent comes from 20 percent of the people.

If those who attend a local church don't support it, who will? If you receive significant spiritual teaching from your local church, shouldn't a significant part of your giving go there?

YOUR FAMILY

> 1 Timothy 5:8: But if anyone does not *provide for his own*, and especially for those of his household, he has denied the faith and is *worse than an unbeliever.*

THE OLD TESTAMENT had laws to protect widows, but what is our role today in caring for widows and family? Paul says the head of the family must *provide for his own*. Don't abdicate your responsibility for the care of your widowed mother or aunt to the church—or the government.

But aren't you responsible for supporting your family anyway, apart from your giving? Of course, but sometimes family members need an extra boost. If your extra help for needy family members advances the gospel, you may consider that as part of your giving. However, supporting family can be never-ending! Set a boundary. Helping family members does not excuse you from generously supporting your church, the poor, or missions.

---

3   Bob Smietana. "Churchgoers Say They Tithe but Not Always to the Church." Lifeway Research. May 10, 2018. https://lifewayresearch.com/2018/05/10/churchgoers-say-they-tithe-but-not-always-to-the-church/

4   Brian Kluth. "State of the Plate 2016." Church Tech Today. December 5, 2016. https://churchtechtoday.com/2016/12/05/state-plate-2016-free-report-infographic/

THE POOR

> Galatians 2:10: They only asked us to *remember the poor*—the very thing I also was *eager* to do.

IN THIS PASSAGE, Paul recounts how the Apostles asked him to *remember the poor* as he preached to the Gentiles, and he is *eager* to help the poor—not reluctant.

At the Last Supper, the disciples mistakenly thought Jesus had instructed Judas to leave the feast and "give something to the poor" (John 13:29). This reveals that Jesus habitually gave to the poor.

Praying for the poor is not enough. Preaching to the poor is not enough. The old saying is true: An empty stomach has no ears.

MISSIONS

> 3 John 7-8: For they went out for the sake of the Name, accepting nothing from the Gentiles. Therefore we ought to support such men, so that we may be *fellow workers with the truth*.

THE EARLY CHURCH sent gospel proclaimers all over the Eastern Mediterranean. By supporting gospel travelers, the believers were *fellow workers with the truth*—true giving partners. As you support gospel workers, you are not "just a donor." You are a *fellow worker with the truth*!

SO WE HAVE four places to give to advance the gospel. How much should we allocate to each one? The New Testament doesn't say. However, regarding the tithe, the New Testament does not teach giving ten percent to the local church. Jesus mentions tithing twice, but neither time does He command it for His followers. Paul taught much about giving, but he was silent on tithing.

In your giving, are these four groups represented? How much should you give to each one? Ask the Lord for His guidance about His money.

Prayer: Father of all, sometimes I don't know where to give. I must help my family, but I need boundaries. I want to be generous with my church too, but I often neglect the poor and missions. Help me honor You in my giving. Give me an idea! Amen.

DAY 13 – AVOIDING THE LOVE OF MONEY

> Now the Pharisees, *who were lovers of money*, were listening to all these things and were scoffing at Him."
>
> –Luke 16:14

IT WAS NOT Jesus who said the Pharisees were *lovers of money.* It was a parenthetical comment by Luke stating what everyone knew! What's puzzling is that the Pharisees were the serious religious people of Jesus' day—exceedingly serious. But they loved money.

In our text today, Jesus has just finished teaching the parable of the unjust steward with the words, "You cannot serve God and wealth" (16:13). We would think that serious religious people would welcome this financial teaching, but not the Pharisees. The phrase *scoffing at Him* literally means "to turn up the nose."

Lest we be too critical, starting in 597 BC with the Jewish exile to Babylon (present-day Iraq), zealous scribes defended the Torah (law of Moses) while Israel was overrun in turn by Babylonians, Persians, Greeks, and finally the Romans. These zealous scribes became the Pharisees—"separated ones." They championed the law of Moses while Israel flirted with Greek and Roman morality.

But despite their zeal for the Old Testament, the 6,000 Pharisees of Jesus' day were known as *lovers of money*. Jesus Himself said the Pharisees "devoured widows' houses" (Matthew 23:14).

The Jews believed financial wealth was a sign of God's blessing. Abraham was rich, Job was rich, and King David was rich. Hence, they scoffed. Theologian Frank L. Cox wrote, "No one scoffs at a scriptural lesson on giving but the lover of money."[5]

This is a stiff warning for us. Just as the serious religious people of Jesus' day drifted toward loving money, so can we—the serious religious people of our day. Being dedicated to Christ and active in Christian activities does not immunize us from the temptation to love money.

Perhaps the love of money is a disguise for *love of power*. Money can surround you with shiny electronic gadgets, fly you first class, and take you to expensive restaurants. And it seems to prove to family and peers that you have finally "made it."

As a former Pharisee, the Apostle Paul understood the lure of money. He said, "Those who *want to be rich* fall into temptation and a snare…" (1 Timothy 6:9). Paul is not writing to money-loving pagans but to money-loving Christians!

In like manner, the writer of Hebrews warned: "Make sure that your character is free from the *love of money*, being content with what you have; for He himself has said, "I will never desert you, nor will I ever forsake you." (Hebrews 13:5, quoting Deuteronomy 31:6).

The antidote to loving money is the promise that *God will never desert nor forsake us*. Friends may forsake us, family may forsake us, and even our stock portfolio can say goodbye—but God will not forsake us. Therefore, relax about seeking money. Don't chase it like a greyhound chases the artificial rabbit at a dog track. Even if he catches it, he has nothing.

We don't know how the serious Pharisees devolved into becoming lovers of money. But as the serious believers of today, we know that we too can be tempted to love money. Martin Luther famously said there are three conversions—the head, heart, and wallet.

5   Frank L. Cox, *According to Luke* (Austin, Texas: Firm Foundation Publishing House, 1941), 50.

Has your wallet been converted?

Albert was a serious Christian in Abuja, Nigeria. As a wealthy businessman, he had a reputation—not as a lover of money but as a lover of people. He regularly invited Christian ministries to use his modest home for meetings, and he provided their meals. When asked why he was so generous Albert replied, "If God owns me, He owns my pockets."

How about you, friend? Does God own your pockets?

> **Prayer:** Lord Jesus Christ, owner of all, I confess that at times I am hungry for the things money can buy. Help me to see money for what it is—a medium of exchange and not the measure of my worth or success. May the phrase *lover of money* not become my reputation. Amen.

DAY 14 – THE SECRET OF SAVING

> There is precious treasure and oil in the dwelling of the wise, but the foolish man swallows it up.
>
> –Proverbs 21:20

IN OUR EARLY years of marriage with a growing family, Alma and I were determined to build a savings account. We deposited our paycheck on Friday, paid our bills, bought groceries, but we were broke by noon Monday—again! Then we'd hold our breath until Friday's paycheck. And we weren't buying crazy stuff! We lived frugally, but we couldn't save.

Most people believe that saving is a good idea, but does anyone say it's easy? Surprisingly, only a few Bible verses commend saving. Our passage today is one of them, and it presents two extremes:

- Wise—foolish
- Accumulation—immediate spending.

The wise have *precious treasure and oil* in their dwellings. How? Because they *accumulate* rather than *swallowing it up*.

Oil refers to olive oil. It was used in food preparation, to soften wounds, and as a trading commodity. Olive trees can live for 500 years, but many trees are required to produce a small amount of oil. Being well-supplied with olive oil was a sign of prosperity.

Because they accumulate, the wise have many economic options. When it comes to spending, they have a small vocabulary: No! But foolish people (including believers) succumb to immediate gratification. They end up with zero economic options.

In an online post about the economy, a young man said, "I cannot find a job that pays enough to make me feel comfortable *given my expenses.*" Hmmm. How about cutting expenses?

Perhaps you know people who have an okay income but are constantly broke. Our passage today does not call them foolish because they are broke but because they do not set aside for the future.

On the other hand, accumulation can be dangerous. Proverbs 21:17 (three verses before today's passage) says, "He who *loves* wine and oil will not become rich." Owning oil may indicate prosperity, but *loving oil* brings poverty. Similar is 1 Timothy 6:10: "The *love of money* is a root of all sorts of evil."

Is it possible to set aside too much? Yes, over-saving is often driven by fear—*what if* I don't have enough? After teaching, "Do not store up for yourselves," Jesus said three times, "Do not worry" (Matthew 6:25–34). Worry is the uninvited domineering guest at the financial planning table.

Also, over-saving keeps you from accomplishing God's strategic purposes in using the resources He has given you.

So when is saving okay? Genesis 41:49 says, "Joseph stored up grain in great abundance like the sand of the sea. ..." But soon came seven years of famine, and "The people of all the earth came to Egypt to buy grain" (Genesis 41:57). Joseph's accumulation had a godly purpose—to help hungry people. If your saving has no specific purpose, you are merely hoarding.

To keep your savings in biblical perspective, ask three questions:

- What are my godly purposes for saving?

- How much accumulation is enough for me to do what I am called to do?

- Is God speaking to me about using some savings for a specific purpose of His right now?

How much to save?

Accumulate enough to accomplish the dreams God has given you—personal dreams, family dreams, and ministry dreams.

Accumulation is necessary. One paycheck won't accomplish your dreams.

Alma and I finally took a scary step regarding our finances.

Rather than trying to save what was left, we decided to save first—the day we were paid. PYF—pay yourself first. We deposited our paycheck on Friday and simultaneously transferred $50 to a savings account. We now had $50 less to spend the next week—I thought we would die. But we didn't!

> **Prayer:** Owner of the cattle on a thousand hills, I recognize my desire for security, but help me avoid the idolatry of worshipping my savings and investments. Are you speaking to me about a specific use of some of my savings now? Guide me to articulate the godly dreams for which I need precious treasure and oil. May I manage my income with discipline rather than swallowing it up. Amen.

DAY 15 – SUPPORTING THE POOR WITH DIGNITY

> You shall not reap to the *very corners of your field*....you shall leave them for the needy and the stranger. I am the Lord your God.
> Leviticus 19:9–10

The Gleaners, Jean-Francois Millet, 1857.
Public Domain.

DOES THIS 3400-YEAR-OLD law for Jewish farmers have any relevance to financial management today, especially if you live in the city and think that Granola grows in Aisle 3 at Trader Joe's?

A similar teaching is Deuteronomy 24:19: "When you reap your harvest in your field and have forgotten a sheaf..., you shall not go back to get it; it shall be for the *alien*, for the *orphan*, and for the *widow, in order that* the Lord your God may *bless you* in *all the work of your hands*."

These passages teach a simple truth—leave some food for the poor. In harvesting, the Jews were not to go after the last stalk of wheat from the corners of their fields, nor retrieve a forgotten sheaf. On their olive trees, the Jews were to shake the boughs only once and leave the unfallen olives for the poor (Deuteronomy 24:20).

These passages run counter to modern Scroogish economic efficiency. A landowner who purchased a 40-acre piece of farm ground bulldozed the trees, asparagus plants and wild blackberry bushes along the fence line, saying, "I've got to squeeze every row of corn I can into this acreage to make it pay."

What must we heed from this ancient rural Jewish law today?

1. Since God cares for those with difficult means of livelihood, so must we. He instituted a law in Israel instructing His people to help the poor by not being so exacting in harvesting. Most governments today have finance policies to help the poor, but often they have unintended negative consequences or destroy dignity. But shall we leave the poor to the government? Why can't believers lead the way in caring for these neglected human beings for whom Christ died?

2. God's provision for the poor was not a handout—the poor went to the fields to glean under the hot sun. Bending down hour after hour picking up fallen grain was (and is) hard work. The physical work of gleaning allowed the poor to retain dignity.

3. As God's people bless the poor, He will bless them in all the work of your hands. He doesn't say how, but you can count on it.

Here are some examples of how we can put this ancient Jewish admonition into practice today:

•   In Lagos, Nigeria, fruit hagglers pass through neighborhoods selling fresh fruit door to door. A friend said he and his wife "haggled hard" to squeeze down the price of the fruit. Recently, they discovered the peddlers profited only a few pennies on each sale. "We felt rebuked," he said. "We no longer try to squeeze them down."

- Waiters and waitresses in restaurants across America dread the "after-church" lunch crowd. Everyone knows that church people tip poorly.

- Years ago, I told a financially frugal friend that I had spent a couple of days negotiating with a car dealer and was able to share the gospel with the sales guy who became a friend. My frugal friend said, "I too recently bought a car, but I haggled so hard I would be embarrassed to say I was a Christian."

At a City Prayer Breakfast in Milwaukee, dignitaries spoke honestly and humbly about the problems of their great city on Lake Michigan. City leaders one by one came to the podium, vowing to work together—especially for the poor.

Then it was time for the Scripture reading. An older Jewish lawyer stood to read Leviticus 19:1–10, our passage today. He slowly read the ancient text and more slowly on the final two verses, "*Don't reap to the very corners of your fields.*" Then he closed the Bible. He scanned the audience of business and religious leaders and said firmly, "Don't try to get the last buck!"

The audience was silent. That day, a 3400-year-old Scripture touched modern man in downtown Milwaukee.

My friend, are you trying to get the last buck? Do you "haggle hard" with vendors? Do you leave meager tips for struggling waitstaff? Are you taking out 75-year-old trees to squeeze in another row of corn?

What quiet actions can you take to help the poor in your world and allow them to retain dignity?

> **Prayer:** Father in Heaven, You care deeply for the poor and disenfranchised. I care too, but I confess that I pick my fields clean—I thrive on economic efficiency. I think more of my bottom line than caring for others. Show me what I can do to provide for the poor in ways that reinforce their dignity. Amen.

DAY 16 – HOW MUCH SALARY IS ENOUGH?

> For John came neither eating nor drinking, and they say, 'He has a *demon*!' The Son of Man came eating and drinking, and they say, 'Behold a *gluttonous* man and a drunkard, a friend of tax collectors and sinners!'
> –Matthew 11:18–19

IMAGINE JOHN THE Baptist and Jesus submitting their budgets for a project with the Village Planning Commission. John comes wearing "a garment of camel's hair" and says his diet is "locusts and wild honey" (Matthew 3:4). John's budget is low. "Too low," say some suspicious commission members.

But Jesus comes wearing a nice seamless tunic (John 19:23). His budget has a huge line item for eating and drinking with tax collectors and sinners (Luke 15:2). "Too high," say some frugal commission members.

How about you? Suppose you submitted your budget to the Planning Commission. How much salary would you ask for? How much is enough?

The culture pushes us to "out-earn" others. John Wesley, the Founder of Methodism, famously said: "Earn all you can, save all you can, give all you can."

Who can argue with that? But earning as much as you can carries a price tag. Do you have the physical and emotional energy to work a second or third job? Will the additional stress affect your health? Your family?

Let's take the emphasis off money and think about our income from Christ's perspective. In the Lord's Prayer, Jesus said, "May Your kingdom come. May Your will be done." What is on Jesus' mind? Advancing the gospel.

In a similar fashion, Paul said, "I do all things for the sake of the Gospel…." (1 Corinthians 9:23). And he told the Philippians: "I know how to live with humble means and I know how to live in prosperity…I can do all things through Him who strengthens me (Philippians 4:11–13).

Instead of striving to earn more and more, how about this guideline?

Earn enough to be at maximum fruitfulness
in the unique calling God has given you.

Your income level is a gospel issue and a personal calling issue more than a money issue. Pastors and missionaries talk about their calling, but we forget that every person on earth is called by God to advance His Kingdom. No one is insignificant.

So, what is *your* life calling? It is broader than your job or career. God has given you certain gifts and placed you in a certain family in a certain geographical place to advance His Kingdom.

Of course, you need to pay off debt and pay your bills on time, and maybe you ought to earn more. And maybe you ought to cut your expenses. But let your calling be your guide. The Almighty Dollar should not be the major factor in finding God's will.

A friend recently took a pay cut with his company to join their human resources department instead of marketing. He felt his gifting and calling had set him up for this, but it dramatically decreased his income. It was a step of faith for both him and his wife.

Seek an income that enables you to accomplish the unique calling God has given you. Never mind what others in your age bracket earn. John the Baptist and Jesus had different incomes, but they both accomplished their callings—and both were criticized.

If you can't be a pine on the top of the hill,
Be a scrub in the valley—but be
The best little scrub by the side of the rill,
Be a bush if you can't be a tree.[6]

---

6   Douglas Malloch, "Be the Best of Whatever You Are," in *The Best Loved Poems of the American People, Selected by Hazel Felleman* (New York: Doubleday, 1936), 102.

Does your income allow you to accomplish your calling? How would you describe your calling?

> **Prayer:** Father in Heaven, sometimes I am caught in the trap of thinking I must be upwardly mobile, earning more and more each year. It's tiring. And striving for money alone is empty. And sometimes I envy those who have more than me. Help me to see beyond my job to the unique calling You have given me. Please supply enough income to enable me to do what You have called me to do. Amen.

DAY 17 – ENJOY YOUR WEALTH! REALLY?

> Instruct those *who are rich* in this present
> world *not to be conceited* or to *fix their hope
> on the uncertainty* of riches, but on God, who
> richly supplies us with *all things to enjoy.*
> —1 Timothy 6:17
> (pastor at Ephesus)

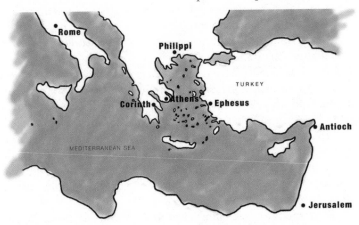

THE EARLY CHURCH attracted the powerless—particularly slaves
and women. But at Ephesus, rich people were also coming to Christ.
Paul's instruction to them is surprising—and an important reminder
for us today.

Ephesus is now a tourist attraction, but in Paul's day, it was
a busy port city of 150,000 on the Turkish coast. Ephesus con-
nected commerce ships from Rome with rich markets in Asia Minor. It even boasted an amphitheater holding 25,000 spectators—a
wealthy Roman city.

And now some of Ephesus' wealthy citizens show up in Timothy's church. Paul doesn't criticize them for being wealthy nor does he admonish them to give it all away (as Jesus instructed the rich young ruler in Matthew 19). But he does tell them what not to do.

First, don't be *conceited*, "high-minded," the old King James language says. The Message Bible says, "full of themselves." People of wealth are often flattered about how wonderful they are—the danger comes when they believe it! Wealthy believers can do things others cannot do, but let no wealthy person think that he is more valuable in the eyes of God than anyone else.

To avoid being "high-minded," a friend in ministry leadership hangs a pair of his dad's striped farm-overalls in his garage where he sees them every day as he leaves for work.

Second, the rich must not *fix their hope on the uncertainty of riches*. One thing is certain—riches are uncertain, as unpredictable as a two-year-old at a family photo shoot. Psalm 62:10 says, "If riches increase, do not set your heart upon them." Wealth is a wonderful tool but a terrible master.

But Paul doesn't leave the Ephesians with only negatives. Now, they are to shift their hope from uncertain riches to what is truly certain—to God who *richly supplies us with all things to enjoy*. Enjoy your wealth! Fine, but isn't that dangerous? We need some background.

In Paul's day, a heresy had infiltrated the churches—Gnosticism, which taught that matter is evil. Only the spirit is good. Because of their "self-abasement and severe treatment of the body" (Colossians 2:23), Gnostic teachers appeared exceedingly holy, and the Ephesians were attracted to them.

Paul spoke against Gnosticism in 1 Timothy 4:3 when he said, "Everything created by God is good...." In Genesis when God created the world, He said that what He had created was "very good" five times (Genesis 1:31). Gnosticism was popular, but it was blatant heresy. And so today—some people pride themselves on having little and they judge others who have more. Gnosticism is not dead.

Paul's word *enjoy* whispers to us about God's love—in contrast to Gnosticism, God wants us to enjoy what He has given us—both spiritual and physical things. The Greek root for *enjoy* is *chara—calm delight*.

But you see the danger. Enjoying material things can lead to worshipping material things—especially the latest electronic gadget! But as we *fix our hope on God*, we can *enjoy—calmly delight* in what

He provides. Let us not trivialize God's love for us.

A young campus minister needed to find a home large enough to host Bible study groups for his growing ministry. Nothing turned up. Finally, by God's grace, just before classes started, He found a fully furnished new home of a professor on leave.

Soon after, the local Methodist pastor came to visit—an older friend. As they sat at the lovely dining room table, the campus pastor began to apologize for the nice furniture and the beautiful tall windows looking out into a woodland.

The minister cut him off and said, "Don't ever apologize for what God has done for you. God gave it—enjoy it!"

> **Prayer:** Father in Heaven, You created matter and called it "very good." Yet sometimes I feel guilty because of the abundance I have compared with others. Help me not to worship the things You have given me but to believe truly that You want me to enjoy what You provide. Amen.

DAY 18 – TWO ADMONITIONS FOR THE WEALTHY—AND A PROMISE

> Instruct them to *do* good, to be *rich* in good works, to be *generous* and *ready to share*, storing up for themselves the *treasure* of a good foundation for the future, so that they may take hold of that which is *life indeed*.
>
> –1 Timothy 6:18-19
> (pastor at Ephesus)

PAUL CONTINUES HIS instruction to wealthy Ephesians with two admonitions, followed by a promise.

1. *Do good, be rich in good works [deeds].* In verse 17 Paul tells them to enjoy what He has given. Now He exhorts them to be rich in good deeds. And good deeds often cost money.

   An Aesop's fable tells of a wealthy miser who buried gold in his garden. Once a week, he dug it up to admire it and then promptly reburied it. One day a robber peeked over his fence and saw the miser reburying his treasure. Later, he slyly returned and stole the miser's precious gold. The next week when the miser came to savor his wealth, he found nothing but an empty hole. The lesson: "Wealth unused might as well not exist."[7]

---

7   Accent on Humor, Murray Milton, Philanthropic Service for Institutions, General Conference of Seventh Day Adventists, 1992, Silver Spring, MD page 26.

2. *Generous and ready to share. Share* is *koinonia*—meaning communion, fellowship or sociable.

In a highbrow cartoon, a wealthy tycoon is sitting in an over-stuffed chair reading his newspaper. A small boy approaches with a toy truck and asks the tycoon to play with him. The rich man replies, "I'm not very good with children. Here's $20."

"Koinonia" implies we give *ourselves*, not merely our money. Giving money is easy compared with giving our hearts.

There's more.

Ready to share means being *emotionally* prepared to give—not someday, but *this day*. It's like buying a car. "Lookers" enjoy car shopping, but they are not emotionally ready to part with their money.

Have you ever had an opportunity to do good, saying to yourself, "I ought to do something," but then got distracted and the moment passed? We are to be *ready to share*—emotionally prepared to give. James, Jesus' brother, said, "But prove yourselves doers of the word, and not merely hearers who delude themselves" (James 1:22).

To put this into practice, a friend of mine prepares a Christmas envelope of cash on December 1. During that busy time of year, he is *ready to share* immediately with the needy.

In addition to the two admonitions, Paul gave a promise—*a treasure for the future*. Jesus used a similar phrase, "treasure in Heaven," three times (Matthew 6:20, 19:21, and Luke 12:33), and that is surely what Paul means here. What is treasure in Heaven? It's certainly more valuable than lottery winnings or free Netflix for eternity.

We know Heaven will be filled with believers "from every nation and all tribes and peoples and tongues standing before the throne and before the Lamb…" (Revelation 7:9). Is it possible *treasure for the future* refers to those people who were helped to Heaven because of your giving?

Think of the welcome you will receive from those who heard the gospel through a missionary you supported. Or a single mom who found Christ because of the Divorce Recovery program in your church. Or the street person who was moved to read the New Testament you gave him along with a McDonald's meal.

This is *life indeed*—doing good, being rich in good works, being generous and ready to share, now and for eternity.

Generosity is not optional. Scottish Bible commentator William Barclay warns, "If Christianity is the best of all religions, then it ought to produce the best of all people." Not misers!

Friend, whether you are wealthy or not, are you "ready to share?" For whom can you do a good deed today?

> **Prayer:** Father in Heaven, compared to most of the world, I am wealthy. Show me today how I can use the resources You have given me to do good for another—a widow with car problems, a discouraged family member, a non-believing friend who is short of cash. May I be generous and ready to share. Amen.

DAY 19 – SUPER-SPIRITUALITY, MONEY AND YOUR PARENTS

> For Moses said, "Honor your father and your mother…" [B]ut you say, "If a man says to his father or his mother, 'whatever I have that would help you is *Corban (that is to say, given to God)*,'" you no longer permit him to do anything for his father or his mother.
>
> –Mark 7:10-12
> (Jesus to the Pharisees)

DO YOUR PARENTS have a financial nest egg laid up for an emergency? What will they do in old age when their income is reduced?

This *Corban Passage* is not well known, but it contains an important warning, especially for godly people, about caring for family.

The Jews cherished the fifth commandment, "Honor your father and your mother" (Exodus 20:12). But over the years, traditions became attached to the Torah like barnacles to a salt-water pier. The *corban* tradition allowed a son to take money allocated for his parents (to help them in old age or illness) and dedicate it to the temple—as a gift. He simply said to his parents, "It is *Corban—given to God*," and he was freed from the obligation to care for them financially.

Why would a son or daughter give to the temple treasury instead of caring for aging parents? Revenge? Perhaps the parents were abusive. To impress others with a show of big giving? To earn a heavenly reward?

Or was it simply greed? The corban gift could be arranged as a trust from which children could earn investment income for themselves.[8] It was a guilt-free *spiritual* way to avoid the expense of

---

8   *Robertson's Word Pictures of the New Testament* (Broadman Press 1932–33. Renewal 1960), https://www.studylight.org/commentaries/rwp/mark-7.html.

caring for parents—and receive income at the same time. Even if the son regretted his decision, the money could not be given back. In the parallel Matthew passage, Jesus called this practice hypocrisy (15:7a).

Paul echoes Jesus. "If anyone does not provide for his own, and especially those of his household, he has denied the faith and is worse than an unbeliever" (1Timothy 5:8). Proverbs 28:24 agrees: "He who robs his father or his mother and says, 'It is not a transgression,' is the companion of a man who destroys."

This is a stiff reminder for adult children who do not discipline their personal spending and, therefore, have little saved for their parents. It is also for those who give large amounts to Christian causes but don't help their parents. "*It is Corban*—given to God. Sorry, Mom and Dad."

Jesus' Corban teaching goes beyond money. A zealous university student was invited to take a Spring Break ministry trip with her campus fellowship, but her parents wanted her to travel with them on a cross-country road trip. Her campus minister advised her to go with her parents since she did not have a good relationship with them—this was her opportunity.

Did she draw closer to her parents? "Not really," she said, "I sat in the back seat reading my Bible and working on my memory verses." She chose spirituality over honoring her parents. Corban indeed!

Similarly, believers who are so busy with church or Bible studies that they fail to communicate with their parents are guilty of *corban* giving.

Of course, putting Christ before people (including family) is what discipleship is all about (Luke 14:26). But in our text today, Jesus chastises those who use *spirituality* as an excuse to neglect their parents.

My friend, what is your strategy to care for your parents when they are no longer able? Are you drifting along hoping emergencies will not come or that your siblings will step up? And are you honoring your parents now by initiating communication with them? By serving them?

Prayer: Father in Heaven, I confess that I sometimes neglect my parents. Please forgive my ungrateful attitude and give me a financial strategy to help my parents in their times of need. And help me to honor them by giving them my time too. No more excuses. Amen.

DAY 20 – GIVING:
SPONTANEOUS OR PLANNED?

Now concerning the *collection* for the saints, as I directed the churches of Galatia, so do you also. On the first day of every week each one of you is to *put aside and save, as he may prosper,* so that no collections be made when I come.

–1 Corinthians 16:1-2

IN KENYA, I was birdwatching on a dusty road with a young Kenyan colleague. He enjoyed pointing out Kenyan birds, even though he owned no binoculars. Soon it was time to head back for our final meeting and my departure home. On a spontaneous whim, I handed him my binoculars and said, "Here, these are yours!" His eyes got big! He broke into a huge smile. I wish you could have seen the delight on his face. And mine! Spontaneous giving is a joy.

Also spontaneously, the Good Samaritan helped a wounded traveler by the side of the road. He bandaged his wounds and gave an innkeeper two denarii, saying, "Take care of him; and whatever more you spend, when I return I will repay you" (Luke 10:35).

But Paul introduces an additional way to give—by design, according to a plan.

The collection for the saints was a major ministry for Paul. The *saints* belonged to the Jewish Mother Church in Jerusalem where the gospel began 20 years previously. After Jesus' resurrection, new believers in Jerusalem were "selling their possessions" and sharing with "anyone who might have need" (Acts 2:45). In those exciting days, there was "not a needy person among them" (Acts 4:34).

Until now! Twenty years later, there were many "needy persons among them." Seeing an opportunity to quiet Jewish suspicions about Gentile converts, Paul invites the Greek Corinthians (map) to support the Jewish believers in Jerusalem—even though they were strangers.

But there was a problem. In the Greek way of giving, wealthy benefactors constructed aqueducts or public buildings—with their names inscribed. Also, the Greeks had a custom called *eranoi*, where citizens gave to a fund to help the unfortunate—but it was a loan, not a gift.

Not to be stopped, Paul exhorts the new Christians to override their cultural traditions. Rather than reaching into their pockets on Collection Day for a spontaneous gift, the Corinthians were to set aside an amount each week.

Setting aside money week-by-week required the Corinthians to think about giving day by day. To use a business term, giving needed to be "top of mind." This would also result in a larger amount given than an unplanned, one-time collection.

What can we learn from Paul's giving instructions?

- **Give with Freedom.** Culture and family heritage are not the final arbiters of your giving decisions.

- **Give First.** *Put aside and save* means that money earmarked for giving is not available for other expenses. When believers don't *first* set aside their giving from their weekly or monthly cash flow, it gets spent on "urgent" needs. "Sorry, Pastor. Sorry Mission Worker. The Lord didn't provide."

What about family emergencies? Follow Paul's advice. *Set aside and save* a "family emergency" amount from each paycheck. If not needed one month, save it until the next.

- **Give Proportionally.** *As he may prosper* shows that giving is based on income. When you earn more, give more. Paul (the former tithing Pharisee) could have instructed the Corinthians to tithe, but he did not.

- **Give with Forethought.** Biblical giving is not haphazard but planned. Sadly, many believers have not formulated a giving plan beyond nebulously supporting their church.

- **Give Frequently.** This collection was a one-time funding event, but the discipline of setting aside an amount for giving each week promotes consistent generosity.

So, should giving be spontaneous or planned? *Both*! Wisely plan your finances so you can give *consistently*. And wisely plan your finances so you can also give *spontaneously*.

> **Prayer:** Lord Jesus Christ, Giver of all. I confess that my giving is sometimes an afterthought—it's not top of mind. Sometimes I can't even remember which missionaries I support. To make giving a part of my discipleship, help me to plan my finances so I can give regularly *and* spontaneously. Amen.

DAY 21 – IS BORROWING A SIN?

> The rich rules over the poor, and the borrower becomes the lender's slave.
> –Proverbs 22:7

THOUGH MANY CONSIDER borrowing a sin, the Bible does not forbid it. Today's verse simply says that if you owe someone money, that someone has control over you—you have another boss.

The Message Bible says, "Don't borrow and put yourself under their power." Similarly, Romans 13:8 says, "Owe nothing to anyone except to love one another…."

Despite these warnings, borrowing is rarely seen as dangerous—even among Christians. In the United States, for those households with credit card debt, the average is $15,482. [9] The average annual interest varies from 12–18%. It will take about nine years for borrowers to pay off their credit card debt if they pay the minimum amount due each month—nine years of bondage! Unfortunately, no one is alarmed.

In Africa, borrowing is not so much via credit cards as from friends or family—"just till I get paid." I was teaching a finance seminar in Zambia to twenty-somethings and asked, "How many of you have loaned money to a friend or family member?" All hands went up. Then I asked, "How many of you are still waiting to be paid back?" All hands went up!

In Asia, a Filipino was asked by a Westerner if borrowing was frowned upon. His humorous answer: "We Filipinos borrow even when we don't need the money!"

For believers, borrowing poses a subtle trap. A veteran missionary revealed what many Christians practice. He admitted, "Borrowing becomes *God's provision* when income is low." Months later, he was deeper in debt. The naïve assumption that "next month God will sup-

---

9   Matthew Frankel. "Nerdwallet's 2017 American Household Credit Card Debt Study." NerdWallet. https://www.nerdwallet.com/blog/average-credit-card-debt-household/.

ply" is a dangerous presumption upon the King of the Universe.

Being in debt increases family pressure. Suppose you borrow to buy a nicer car—only because you want a nicer car. The extra payments stretch your finances, so you take a second job, which adds family pressure. Frustration rises. Arguments are more frequent. At wit's end, you can think of nothing except escaping. Like the writer in Psalm 55:22, you wish for *wings like a dove to fly away*!

What if you can't repay? Psalm 37:21 says, "The wicked borrows and does not pay back, but the righteous is gracious and gives." It may not be a sin to borrow, but it certainly is a sin not to repay. Do you want to be known as "wicked?"

But there's more. Borrowing strains relationships—as happened with two brothers, "Zach" and "Carl."

> Zach lost his job and found himself three months behind on mortgage payments. He asked his brother Carl for a loan. Though hesitant, Carl stretched his finances and loaned Zach $3,000. Zach promised to pay it back.
>
> Years passed, but there was no repayment. Carl reminded Zach, but it was awkward. The brothers stopped communicating.
>
> Finally, at a family reunion, Zach (with tears) admitted to Carl that he was broke. On the spot, Carl and his wife graciously decided to cancel the $3,000 loan— it was now a gift. Zach was grateful, and Carl had a deep sense of peace.
>
> Five weeks later, Zach invited Carl and his son for a fishing weekend—a nice way to rekindle their relationship. At the lake, Zach announced that he had a surprise—a new bass boat!
>
> Carl said later, "Zach found money to buy a bass boat, but he couldn't find money to repay me! I was so angry!"

The saying is true: Before borrowing money from a friend, decide which you need more—the money or your friend. Mark Twain wrote: "Friendship…can last a lifetime, unless you try to borrow money."

In summary, debt: (1) gives you another master, (2) adds financial pressure, and (3) strains relationships. Avoid it!

My friend…

- For what specific item are you tempted to borrow? Why not save and pay cash for it?

- Do you owe money? How quickly can you pay it back? Instead of your daily Starbucks treat, set that money aside to repay—and keep a friend.

- Is someone asking to borrow from you? Instead of loaning, can you make it a gift?

> **Prayer:** Father of all, I confess that I am tempted to borrow money for stuff I can probably get along without. Please help me pay off my debts now and avoid the temptation to borrow again. I don't want to be a slave to anyone except You. Amen.

DAY 22 – SEVEN FINANCIAL WORDS TO PRAY DAILY

Give us this day our daily bread.
–Matthew 6:11

The Lord's Prayer, James Tissot, between 1886 and 1894. Public Domain.

THE LORD'S PRAYER contains six requests. We are so familiar with Jesus' prayer that we overlook the fourth request, which is surprisingly earthy. Here's an overview: The first three requests are about God and His Kingdom; the keyword is *Your*:

1. May *Your* name be hallowed.

2. May *Your* kingdom come.

3. May *Your* will be done.

The second three requests are about **us**:

1. Give *us* our daily bread.

2. Forgive *us* our debts.

3. Lead *us* not into temptation (including deliver us from evil).

Requests #1–3 are theological, #5 is relational, and #6 is moral. But the fourth request is about physical life. Jesus, the Son of God, the most spiritual man who ever lived, is concerned about physical bread.

Two chapters earlier on the Mount of Temptation in Matthew 4:4, Jesus told the devil, "Man shall *not* live on bread alone, but on every word that proceeds from the mouth of God." Throughout history, super-spiritual ascetics lived meagerly, starving themselves to achieve holiness. They concluded that bread was not important. But Jesus did not say, "Man shall not live on bread *at all*."

Jesus honors the physical-ness of our existence. We are "fearfully and wonderfully made" (Psalm 139:14)—and that includes a need for bread.

Bread, as used here, signifies the necessities of life. This request affirms the profound but simple theological truth that Jesus was fully human, and so are we. Jesus taught us to pray for our physical necessities. However, we pray for *daily bread*, not *daily cake*, as humorously expressed by Dale Bruner in *Matthew, a Commentary*.

Nor does Jesus say, "Give us a 12-month supply of bread." Only for today. As we pray "this day," we acknowledge our dependence on the Lord "this day" and every day.

Note also that the Lord's prayer is corporate—*our* daily bread, not *my* daily bread. Besides ourselves, let us ask bread for those without bread. And let us ask how we can help them. This seven-word request pushes us to think about others.

Finally, this prayer is addressed to our Father in Heaven—our true Source. Jesus lifts our eyes to the skies—beyond our paycheck. No matter how secure your employment nor how large your investment portfolio, they could blow away like dandelion fluff in a summer wind. You have no control over a volatile employer or a volatile economy.

A missionary was talking to a friend outside their church one Sunday morning. The friend asked the missionary if he raised personal support or if he was funded by his agency. The missionary said that he raised support, then piously added, "I trust God for my income."

The friend paused a moment, then said, "I own a printing company with three employees, and I too trust God for my income." Touche'!

With seven words, Jesus points us to Heaven. Rich or poor, let us pray these seven words every day—specifically asking for our physical needs—food for today, a better job, new clients, school fees for our kids. Let us not trust in our job skills, our employer, or the economy but *daily* ask our faithful Father for bread. He is the Source.

Back of the bread is the snowy flour;
And back of the flour the mill.
And back of the mill is the wheat and the shower,
And the sun and the Father's will.

–M.D. Babcock

Prayer: Father in Heaven, I confess I neglect to look to You every day as my Source. But now I ask You anew for daily bread—for the physical necessities I need to do Your will today. And please show me what I can do to assist others in my world who are without bread. Amen.

DAY 23 – RECAPTURING CHEERFUL GIVING

> Each one must do just as he has *purposed in his heart*, not *grudgingly or under compulsion*, for God loves a *cheerful* giver.
> –2 Corinthians 9:7

YOU KNOW THIS verse—"God loves a *cheerful* giver." In the Greek, *cheerful* is *hilaros*—*hilarious* in English. But here's the reality: Though most believers are not *joyless* givers, they're not *joyful* givers either. Their giving brings them the same joy as paying a parking fine.

And with electronic giving replacing the offering basket or writing checks, givers become emotionally detached—they can't remember what or whom they support. And if one spouse handles the finances, it's even worse. They are not joyless—just neutral.

How can we recapture the joy of cheerful giving? Insert these guidelines from today's passage into your giving practices.

1. *Purposed in his heart* implies choosing deliberately—the decision is yours. In his heart reveals that giving decisions ought not to be purely academic. When God commanded Israel to build a tabernacle in the desert, He said: "Tell the sons of Israel to raise a contribution for Me; from every man whose heart moves him." (Exodus 25:2).

   Recently, I "felt" I should send $40 to a friend whose wife had just been diagnosed with cancer. This $40 was above and beyond our giving plan—a decision of the heart. "Go out for lunch," I said in my note. They loved it, and I loved doing it. I was joyful!

2. *Not grudgingly.* The Greek *ek lupe* means "out of sorrow"—reluctantly. Giving reluctantly is like having a

tearful bon voyage party for your dollars when you pull them out of your wallet, saying regretfully, "Goodbye old friends."

Perhaps Paul was thinking of Deuteronomy 15:10, where the Jews were commanded to give to the poor: "Your heart shall not be grieved when you give to him."

3.   [Not] *under compulsion*. Many believers feel obligated to give a certain percentage of their income, but they give *under compulsion*.

Similarly, a generous believer was frustrated: "I get tons of appeals—missionaries needing support, the teen pregnancy center is building an addition, and Sunday at church. It's never-ending." Because he was generous, he got even more appeals, and he couldn't say no. As a result, he supported many causes with token amounts. He felt *obligated* and was becoming resentful.

I told him, "You don't have to give to every appeal. 'No' is a complete sentence."

This is also a reminder for ministry leaders. Are you subtly coercing people to give? Saying things like, "Christians spend more on dog food than they give to missions." Or, "You need to give back to the church after all the church has done for you." And so on.

A missionary asked a giving partner to increase his support, saying apologetically, "You probably get 'hit up' a lot." The partner said, "I don't have a ton of money, but I love being asked. It shows me good things are going on for God. I feel free to say yes or no."

Cheerful giving is captured in a classic story about British author Thomas Carlyle (1795–1881). When Carlyle was a boy, a beggar came to his house while his parents were gone:

"On a boyish impulse [Carlyle] broke into his own savings-bank and gave the beggar all that was in it, and he tells us that never before or since did he know such sheer happiness as came to him in that moment."[10]

10   William Barclay, *The Daily Bible Study Series, The Letters to the*

How about you? What describes your giving?

- Joyless, resentful
- Feel obligated to give to every need—not sure why
- Neutral, detached
- Neglectful, don't think about it much
- Guilty
- Cheerful

Theologically speaking, God loves resentful and neutral givers too, but wouldn't you like to recapture the joy of giving like young Thomas Carlyle? Slow down and ask your heart: To what do I desire to give? To whom do I desire to give? What can I do to enjoy my giving?

Prayer: Father in Heaven, I don't think I'm joyless in my giving—I'm just neutral or neglectful. Giving is not daily on my mind. Help me to be more attentive in my giving. I choose now to give with cheerfulness. Amen.

Corinthians (Philadelphia: The Westminster Press, 1954), 262.

DAY 24 – THE IMPORTANT ROLE OF MONEY IN YOUR SPIRITUAL GROWTH

> Therefore if you have not been *faithful* in the use of *unrighteous wealth*, who will entrust the *true riches* to you?
>
> –Luke 16:11

TODAY'S PASSAGE GIVES a surprising teaching about how to handle *unrighteous wealth*—money included. Here are two historically opposing viewpoints about material things.

The Ascetic Simeon Stylites, artist unknown. Public Domain.

In the first century, the Gnostics sect declared that since God is holy, matter is evil. Only the spiritual is important. Accordingly, some early Church Fathers lived as desert hermits in an attempt to draw closer to God. Simeon Stylites of Syria (390?–459) lived on tall pillars (drawing) for 30 years and preached to crowds from elevated platforms.[11]

By contrast, in the early 1900s, some Christian groups began to teach that you should pray for wealth because it demonstrates God's hand upon you. "God wants you healthy and God wants you wealthy," they said then and still say today.

Most of us live somewhere between Simeon Stylites and late-night wealth evangelists. Is there a happy medium? No. Rather than going to the extremes of rejecting or seeking unrighteous wealth, we need a different mindset as shown by today's passage.

First, what exactly are *true riches*? Jesus doesn't explain, but in our passage today, He contrasts *true riches* with *unrighteous wealth*. *True riches* surely include non-material things like biblical truth, the eternal souls of men and women, and "the unfathomable riches of Christ" (Ephesians 3:8).

Second, we get a surprise. We receive *true riches* based on how we *use* non-true riches—*unrighteous wealth*. Instead of eschewing riches or desperately seeking riches, we are to faithfully manage riches, that which we *can* see—the physical. Then we will be entrusted with things we *can't* see, *true riches*.

But many believers have a semi-Gnostic relationship with material things. As a new believer in Christ, I was deeply impressed by our godly Bible-study leader who rightly warned us against materialism. He said, "Material things? They're all going to burn."

He was right. According to prophecies in Revelation, material things (along with the earth) will burn *one day*. But *this day—today*, the way we handle *unrighteous wealth* is our passport to receiving something more valuable—*true riches*. Material things are a litmus test. If we faithfully manage material things, we receive *true riches*.

The issue is stewardship. We are not owners, but caretakers of what God puts into our hands. We flippantly say, "*My* computer, *my* house, *my* body," but they are not truly *mine*. Haggai 2:8 says, "The silver is mine and the gold is mine, says the Lord."

---

11   Will Durant, *The Age of Faith* (New York: Simon and Schuster, 1950), 60.

That's why we pray over financial decisions: "Lord, do *You* want me to upgrade *Your* computer? Shall I put a new roof on *Your* house?"

How do we know if we are faithfully managing material things? Two indicators pop out in parables Jesus told before and after today's text.

Preceding our text is Jesus' story of the "Unrighteous Steward" who cheated his landlord (16:1-9). The landlord sacked him for dishonesty.

Following our text is Jesus' story of the rich man who lived "in splendor every day" (16:19–31) but ignored poor Lazarus who begged at his gate, "covered with sores." Both men died. The rich man ended up in Hades while Lazarus found himself in Abraham's bosom. If wealth was a sign of God's blessing, why was the rich man in Hades?

These two stories highlight poor stewardship. The property manager cheated his employer. The rich man ignored human suffering. Neither managed *unrighteous wealth* according to God's values—absolute honesty and compassionate generosity. And neither received *true riches*.

My friend, do you want *true riches*? Do you long to have a spiritual ministry to your family and friends? To grow in intimacy with God? To understand the Bible? Start today by *faithfully* handling the material resources God has put into your hands. And do it with absolute honesty and compassionate generosity.

If you handle well that which you *can see*, God will entrust you with something you *cannot see*—*true riches*.

Prayer: Dear Master, sometimes I forget that what You have placed in my hands is actually Yours. Help me not to love money nor to disdain it. May I faithfully manage the *unrighteous wealth* You have given me—may I be honest and generous. As it pleases You, may I receive *true riches*. Amen.

DAY 25 – WHY DID JESUS DIRECT HIS DISCIPLES TO TRAVEL WITHOUT MONEY?

> Do not *acquire gold*, or silver, or copper for your money belts, or a bag for your journey, or even two coats, or sandals, or a staff; for the *worker is worthy of his support*. And whatever city or village you enter, *inquire* who is worthy in it, and stay at his house until you leave that city.
>
> –Matthew 10:9-11

HOW DO WE put this puzzling passage into practice? No preparations? Really?

Jesus is instructing the Twelve about a short-term mission trip. They are not to go to Samaria (map) nor to the Gentiles (Matthew 10:5–6) but only to the "lost sheep of the house of Israel." What provisions are they to take—none! Go as you are!

When St Francis of Assisi (1181–1226) heard this, he abandoned his shoes and went barefoot.

But when your church sends short-term missionaries, every night's lodging is pre-arranged. They will wear shoes and take extra cash, extra clothing,

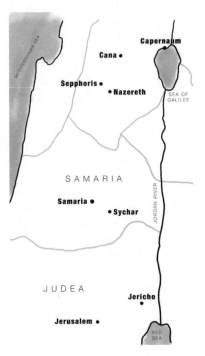

two giant bags of Gummi Bears, and a favorite pillow.

Some background is helpful.

- Taking no money was not unusual since, by custom, the Jews were required to host traveling rabbis.

- *Acquiring gold* as a recompense for ministry might mark the Twelve as money-hungry charlatans.

- Why no bag? Jews typically carried bags for supplies, but the Greek word *peran* also means "beggar's bag." Jesus did not want His workers to adopt a beggar's mentality.

- Two coats and [extra] sandals? The outer coat could be used as a covering for sleeping outside overnight. But Jesus intended His workers to spend their nights with worthy hosts—not outside. No extra sandals implied a short trip. Go as you are.

- Why no staff? A staff denoted authority—such as Moses' rod. Also, some staffs contained a secret compartment for coins.

- Jesus established a precedent for missions in verse 11: *The worker is worthy of his [or her] support.* Twenty years later, the Apostle Paul quoted this principle in 1 Corinthians 9:14 and 1 Timothy 5:18, "The laborer is worthy of his wages."

But there's more. During His final night with the Twelve (immediately following the Last Supper), Jesus recalls sending them out with no provisions. "Did you lack anything?" He asked. "No, nothing," they replied. "But now," He says, "whoever has a money belt is to take it along." (Luke 22:35–38).

In Matthew 10 they were not to prepare, but now they are to prepare. What's the difference? Length of time and type of audience.

In Matthew 10, the disciples were on a short mission going to Jews only—not cross-culturally to Samaritans or Gentiles. Now, with the resurrection looming and the Great Commission about to be given, Jesus will send them to the world—cross-culturally—for the rest of their lives. Now they must prepare. Different audiences and different timelines require different strategies.

These instructions give us a glimpse into how Jesus thinks. As giving partners, we must understand that:

1. Jesus puts us in situations where we must depend on Him. Never mind that we feel helpless and uncomfortable. Comfort is not Jesus' chief concern.

2. Pompous trappings and authoritative accoutrements (like a walking staff) are not Jesus' style. Speak out against mission extravagance and pretentious authority when you see it so the gospel will not be hindered.

3. Jesus wants His workers to involve giving partners, but they are not to beg nor have the demeanor of a beggar. Jesus' workers are "worthy of support."

When you support long-term, cross-cultural mission workers, make sure they are fully provisioned in finances, prayer, and logistics.

And when it's your turn to speak for the gospel to a colleague or neighbor, remember, God can use you just as you are—even if you feel uncomfortable or ill-prepared. You don't need a staff!

Prayer: Lord Jesus, I have opinions about how ministry should be funded. I now yield to Your guidelines. And in my personal ministry, I confess I like being comfortable. Help me to go to my friends without pomp and without authority—just as I am, trusting You. Amen.

DAY 26 – WHY DIDN'T JESUS TELL EVERYONE TO ABANDON THEIR RICHES?

> And Jesus said to him, "If you wish to be complete, go and *sell your possessions* and give to the poor, and you will have treasure in Heaven; and *come follow me*." But when the *young man* heard this statement, he went away *grieving*; for he was one who *owned much property*.
>
> –Matthew 19: 21–22
> (to the rich young ruler)

JESUS TOLD THIS *young man* to sell his possessions and give to the poor, but He didn't ask that of others.

For example, in calling Matthew, the tax collector, Jesus ignored his wealth. Fishermen Peter and Andrew were called to become "fishers of men" with no suggestion of dumping assets. Indeed, Peter still had a fishing boat after the resurrection (John 21:4). And though wealthy Zacchaeus volunteered to give half his possessions, there is no record that Jesus suggested it.

So why is the man in our text today told to give it all? What do we know of him?

From Matthew, we learn that he was young, from Luke that he was a ruler and "extremely rich," and from Mark that Jesus "felt a love for him"—this now famous "rich young ruler."

He seemed to be a God-seeker, asking Jesus in verse 16, "What good thing shall I do" to obtain eternal life? *Do!* Not what he should know or what he should believe but what he should *do*. Perhaps a nice gift for Jesus' ministry would assure eternal life? That he could *do*.

Going to the heart of the matter, Jesus said, "Keep the commandments," and then He listed five of the Ten Commandments dealing with relationships—murder, adultery, stealing, lying, and honoring parents. Did Jesus think that the young man had relationship problems—perhaps he had taken advantage of poor people to gain wealth?

But the rich young ruler brashly answered in verse 20, "All these things I have kept." Then he asked, "What am I still lacking?" Despite obeying the law, he honestly admitted that he had no assurance of eternal life.

Now Jesus jumps from theology to economics: *Sell your possessions and give to the poor*. Surprised by this point-blank assault, we can imagine the shocked young man took a step backward, his eyes narrowed, an eyebrow arched. Silence. The disciples and bystanders were astounded. Weren't wealthy people the most blessed by God?

But Jesus didn't linger on a negative. He replaced the man's potential loss of wealth with His Presence, saying, "Come, follow Me." Perhaps the young man pondered Jesus' invitation for a moment, but finally, he *went away grieving*. He chose wealth over companionship with Christ (and assurance of salvation).

So why did Jesus admonish him to give everything? We have a clue—*he went away grieving; for he was one who owned much property*. His property was his idol—#1 in his life. It was more important to him than assurance of eternal life.

Luke 14:33 says, "None of you can be My disciple who does not give up all his own possessions." Christ first! For everyone.

Putting Christ first is simple, but not easy. A missionary to Brazil said, "Surrendering to Christ is like being surrounded by God's love in your secret hideout. And finally, you step outside with your hands up." Over my years of discipleship mentoring in the marketplace, I find that those who struggle with assurance of salvation carry a secret idol—something besides Christ is #1. Often money. Other idols might be career or family or reputation or pornography or gambling. Or the fear of change.

But we need not focus on what we give up. After we surrender, Jesus invites us to follow Him and enjoy His companionship—into eternity with 100% assurance. *Let us not go away grieving.*

Prayer: Father in Heaven, I want to be 100% certain of Heaven, but I confess I have a secret idol. Please help me day by day to surrender that which stands between You and me—especially money, property, and material things. Thank you for loving me like You did the rich young ruler. I do not want to walk away *grieving*. Amen.

DAY 27 – YOUR GIVING: INSTANT GRATIFICATION OR DELAYED GRATIFICATION?

> So *when you give* to the poor, do not sound a trumpet before you, as the hypocrites do in the synagogues and in the streets, so *that they may be honored by men.* Truly I say to you, *they have their reward in full.* But when you give to the poor, do not let your left hand know what your right hand is doing, so that your giving will be in secret; and your Father who *sees what is done in secret will reward you.*
>
> –Matthew 6:2-4

IT IS EASY to criticize the hypocrites of Jesus' day for showing off their giving in the synagogues and in the streets.

Lest we be too hard on the hypocrites (or ourselves), note that Jesus did not criticize their desire for recognition. Being made in God's image, we are not inert substances able to live without recognition.

But our legitimate desire for recognition has been hijacked by our sinful nature—we want to be noticed ("seen" NIV) not only by God but also by people—especially certain people. The desire to be noticed can become an addiction that controls every action and thought—so desirous are we of an approving smile.

Is recognition unimportant to you? Then how do you feel when your colleague is applauded for work you did behind the scenes?

Given that we need some kind of recognition, what is Jesus teaching *when you give?*

1. Giving to impress others brings a *reward*, but it is fleeting. Jesus does not say that those who trumpet their giv-

ing receive no reward. He said, *"They have their reward in full."* Your reward is a few fleeting seconds of adulation from others—a momentary good feeling. Enjoy that smile from your pastor because that's your reward in *full*. You're done.

2. Giving secretly to the Lord brings a *reward*—but it is undefined.

"Your Father who *sees* what is done in secret will *reward* you." Even when no one else notices, your giving in secret is seen by your Father. And He *will reward you*.

The Greek word for reward is *misthos*—pay for service, wages. *Misthos* is also used in Hebrews 11:6: "God is a *rewarder* of those who diligently seek Him." God is not a busy, harried despot who is too preoccupied to notice your service. He sees and He rewards. Count on it. But He doesn't say what the reward is.

We are left with two choices: An immediate fleeting reward from people or an undefined reward from God. As easy as this choice seems, wanting to please people still haunts us.

The Apostle Paul was tempted by the desire to impress others. He asks bluntly, "Am I now seeking the favor of men, or of God? Or am I *still trying* to please men?" (Galatians 1:10). "Still trying" implies he had struggled with people-pleasing.

To combat people-pleasing, identify those people you are trying to impress—it is not 2,500! It is only two or three—a disapproving parent, a skeptical boss, a friend from school who is now wealthy. Identify them. Why do you long for their approval?

Let us stop blowing our little trumpets. Longing for recognition from people reveals at whom we are looking. It shows how little we seek the Father. Invite Him alone to be your Rewarder. *Your Father who sees what is done in secret will reward you.*

Prayer: Father in Heaven, I confess I sometimes long to sound a trumpet to show certain people what a good person I am. But You see my giving and my behind-the-scenes service for You. I need no other reward than knowing You know. Amen.

DAY 28 – HOW MUCH SHOULD CHRISTIAN WORKERS BE PAID?

> The elders who *rule well* are to be considered worthy of *double honor*, especially those who work hard at preaching and teaching. For the *Scripture says*, "You shall not muzzle the ox while he is threshing," and "The laborer is worthy of his wages."
>
> –1 Timothy 5:17–18
> (overseer at Ephesus)

QUIZ: WHAT PERCENT of American pastors work part-time jobs because of inadequate compensation?

- 10%
- 25%
- 80%

The answer is 80%, and it is higher in African-American churches.[12] Similarly, in Africa and Asia, most pastors cannot survive without side employment. "Poor as a church mouse" is a proverb. But where is it written that Christian leaders should be paid poorly? One church board deliberately paid its pastor less than the salary of the lowest paid board member.

There are exceptions. Some churches pay their pastors extravagantly since they believe it demonstrates God's blessing.

The Bible doesn't give specifics about paying Christian workers, but eight words from our passage today reveal a counter-cultural guideline. Fasten your seatbelt.

---

12   https://baptistcourier.com/2016/11/bivocational-ministry-new-normal/

1. *Rule well, work hard:* A first-grade student was asked what he wanted to be when he grew up. He replied, "I want to be a preacher at church. I'd only have to work one hour per week."

    The church at Ephesus had grown to the point of needing ruling elders and preaching elders—who surely worked more than one hour per week. Paul doesn't say all elders should receive double honor—only those who *rule well* or *work hard* at preaching and teaching.

    This is a reminder to pastors and mission-workers. Being called to ministry does not give you permission to be lackadaisical. Are you *ruling well*? Do you *work hard*? Those who support you work hard!

2. *Double honor.* The Greek word is *timao*, a financial term meaning "price or value." *Timao* does not mean "rhetorical honor." Presenting your leaders with plaques at banquets does not atone for paying them poorly.

    The exact meaning of *double honor* is a mystery. It might refer to paying double what church widows at Ephesus were paid for their informal part-time ministry (1 Timothy 5:3–16). Though undefined, the implication is clear: Be generous to those who work hard in ministry.

3. *Scripture says.*

    It is not merely Paul's opinion that pastors should be paid well. He quotes Moses and Jesus to punctuate his exhortation—and he calls their words *Scripture*. Notice that Paul equates Jesus' words as *Scripture* along with the Old Testament.

    Deuteronomy 25:4 commanded the Jews not to muzzle their oxen as they walked in circles threshing out grain (separating the grain from the stalks). Let them dip their heads down to munch some grain. This verse is also quoted in our kitchen to justify pre-dinner sampling.

    And then Paul quotes Jesus from Luke 10:7—"The laborer is worthy of his wages." When Jesus sent the

Twelve and the Seventy to minister in the cities of Israel, they were to inquire for hosts to support them. Though inexperienced in ministry, the disciples *were worthy of their wages.*

If you are a gospel minister who works hard, this passage affirms you—whatever *double honor* means, you are worthy of it! Unfortunately, some missionaries are too timid to go after a full budget. And some pastors hesitate to ask for a much-needed raise.

If you are in ministry as a career, how would your work be better if you had adequate pay? How would your home life be better if you had adequate pay? Your pay is not about you—it is about the advancement of the gospel.

My friend, if you support missionaries, be generous. If you serve on a mission committee, this passage exhorts you to pay God's messengers generously. And that includes your pastor!

Prayer: Father of all, the religious culture is squeamish about discussing ministry and money. Help me speak up for the generous support of Your workers. And help me to be generous to the gospel workers You have put in my world. Amen.

DAY 29 – IS YOUR GOAL TO BE SUCCESSFUL?

> He who is *faithful in a very little thing*
> is *faithful* also in much; and he who
> is unrighteous in a very little thing is
> unrighteous also in much.
>
> –Luke 16:10

A FEW YEARS ago after picking up our clothes at the dry cleaners, I discovered a small plastic bag pinned to my dress pants. It contained a coin—a 25-cent piece. "The dry cleaners found it in my trousers," I figured.

I returned to the store two weeks later and brought the 25-cent piece with me—still in the plastic bag. I showed it to the young, hard-working shop owner saying, "It wasn't necessary to return this coin, I would not have missed 25 cents. But you took the trouble to put it in a plastic bag and return it—why?"

The owner seemed embarrassed. He said, "I had to return it. It wasn't mine."

Amazing—here at the Academy Street Dry Cleaners was a living example of *faithfulness in a very little thing*—the theme of our passage today.

In the Greek and Roman culture of Jesus' day, my 25-cent coin would not have been returned. Blogger Adrian Vrettos at www.athensguide.com said, "Being caught with your fingers in the till was so common that ancient Greek historians [expressed] wonder about the one or two cases where men…were actually straight in their dealings."

So widespread was dishonesty, the Greek philosopher Diogenes went about holding a lantern to men's faces searching for an honest man. In Rome, prestigious senate candidates openly gave cash in exchange for votes. Few considered it wrong.

Against this backdrop, Jesus teaches absolute faithfulness in small things. *Faithful* is the Greek *pistos*—trustworthy, reliable. It is used 56 times in the New Testament—an important word in the Christian faith. It appears in the passages below.

> In one of Jesus' parables, a landowner entrusted five talents to his servant. After the servant gained five additional talents, the master said, "Well done, good and *faithful* slave, you were *faithful* in a few things, I will put you in charge of many things; enter into the joy of your master (Matthew 25:23)." Because of the servant's faithfulness *in a few things*, he was given more responsibility and was welcomed to a joyful relationship with his master.
>
> The Apostle Paul agrees: "It is required of stewards that one be found *trustworthy*" (1 Corinthians 4:1). It's not optional.
>
> 1 Thessalonians 5:24 says, "Faithful is He who calls you, and He also will bring it to pass." God is our model of being trustworthy. He is not capricious or whimsical like the manmade gods of mythology. Because He demonstrates faithfulness—reliability—honesty, we can trust Him.

As Christians, are we different from the ancient Greeks and Romans? Are we different from today's secular culture? Would Diogenes find an honest person in your workplace? In your church? Today, it is common to:

- Fib a little on our income tax and fudge a little on our golf score

- Take stuff home from our workplace—pens, postage stamps, kitchenware

- Forget to reimburse the office copy machine for personal use

- Keep extra change mistakenly given by a harried checkout lady at the grocery

My friend, let us be different! Let us set higher standards. How can we be reliable in big things if we have a habit of being unreliable in little things?

Our passage does not say, "He who is *successful* in a very little thing…." You are not called to be successful; you are called to be faithful. Even when you work hard, you won't always be successful, but you can always be faithful—trustworthy—reliable.

At the end of our lives when the Lord welcomes us to eternity, He will not ask, "Were you successful?" Instead, He will say, "Well done, good and *faithful* servant."

Prayer: Father in Heaven, You hold us to high standards, but You do not demand the impossible, like 100 percent success. But I love success! Help me to be *faithful* to You and to Your people in all I do—both in small things and big things. Amen.

DAY 30 – IS YOUR GIVING AN OPTIONAL ADD-ON?

> But just as you abound in everything, in faith and utterance and knowledge and in all earnestness and in the love we inspired in you, see that you abound in this *gracious work* also.
>
> —2 Corinthians 8:7

THE CORINTHIANS *abounded* in five important aspects of the Christian life—trusting God, sharing their faith (utterance), possessing spiritual insights, taking their faith seriously (earnestness), and loving others. Now Paul exhorts them to abound in one thing more, *this gracious work*—the Collection for Jerusalem. Giving!

Paul could have exhorted the Corinthians merely to *give*, but he chose the word *abound*. In Greek it is perisseuo—"to super-abound, beyond measure, excess, excel." Perisseuo was the word used to describe the many leftover broken pieces after Jesus fed the multitude (Mark 8:8).

Exhorting the Corinthians to abound in giving was risky since the young Corinthian church was struggling with growing pains. A quick glance at 1 Corinthians shows:

- A spirit of rivalry and jealousy among loyalists to Apollos, Peter, and Paul

- Sexual immorality

- Taking one another to secular courts of law

- Confusion about marriage

- Eating meat offered to idols

There's more. A year previously, these zealous Corinthians had agreed to give toward the Collection for Jerusalem (2 Corinthians 8:10). But they had not followed through. Would Paul's bold reminder be well received?

Given the troubles in Corinth, you and I might have dropped the subject of following through on giving, but not Paul! *Abound* in giving, he says.

Paul wants the Corinthians to understand that generous giving is an essential "basic" of the Christian life, not an optional add-on. Without the life-giving outlet of generous giving, the Corinthians were in danger of becoming self-occupied—like a stream becoming a dead-end swamp.

The Corinthians needed an outlet, and so do we.

But today, generosity is often an optional add-on—even for serious Christians. Why is generous giving neglected?

- I never have "extra money."

- I give my time—isn't that enough?

- I tithe—isn't that enough?

- Electronic giving is sterile; I don't even realize I am giving.

- I'll give more when I make it through the problems I am facing.

- Busyness—I don't think about giving unless I am asked.

Another obstacle is that many Christians treat giving like bill paying. They don't see giving as vertical. They don't see giving as an honor.

In the book, *Letters to Scattered Pilgrims,* author Elizabeth O'Connor describes the honor of giving.

The deacons of a small congregation in Virginia told their pastor that a widow with six children was giving $4 each month to the church. Since the widow was in economic difficulty, the deacons advised the pastor to tell her that she was relieved of the burden of giving.

In the pastor's words: "As I [explained the concern of the deacons], tears came into [the widow's] eyes. 'I want to tell you,' she said, 'that you are taking away from me the last thing that gives my life dignity and meaning.'"

A horizontal view of giving (like that of the deacons above) leaves God out. Giving is first vertical—between you and God. Abounding in giving is not merely defined by how much you give. Abounding in giving includes seeing giving as an honor—like the Virginia widow. That brings dignity.

My Friend,

- Are you *abounding* in giving? Is generosity an essential "basic" in your walk with Christ?

- Do you see giving generously as an *honor* or more like bill-paying?

- How can you incorporate *abounding* generosity into your daily life?

Besides Paul, giving is extremely important to God. The classic Bible verse on giving is one you know—John 3:16: "God so loved the world He *gave....*"

> **Prayer:** Father in Heaven, You are the Chief Giver of all. You gave us physical life, and You left Heaven to live among us and sacrifice Yourself for us. Help me to *abound* in giving—and to make it a *basic* in my life with You. Amen.

DAY 31 – OVERLY CONSCIENTIOUS GIVING

The Pharisee stood and was praying this *to himself*: "God, I thank you that I am not like other people: swindlers, unjust, adulterers, or even like this tax collector. I fast twice a week; I pay tithes on *all* that I get."
But the tax collector, standing some distance away, was even unwilling to lift up his eyes to Heaven, but was beating his breast saying, "God, be merciful to me, the sinner!"

–Luke 18:11-13

The Pharisee and the Publican, James Tissot, between 1886 and 1894. Public Domain.

THIS PHARISEE WENT up to the temple to pray, but he did not pray to God—he prayed *to himself* about his pious character and his track record in fasting and giving. He ate little and gave much! God was lucky to have him.

About this Pharisee, three things must be said.

1. He was conscientious. Though we loathe complimenting self-righteous people, we must at least credit him with faithfulness to the Old Testament rule of tithing. By contrast, the Jewish people were *not* historically faithful in tithing. The Levites (the temple staff who received the tithes) frequently had to leave their ministry to work in the fields.

2. He was a self-righteous over-achiever. He tithed on *all* that he received. But the Old Testament required tithes only on income from grains, new wine, oil, and first-born livestock (Leviticus 27:30). In tithing *all that I get*, he considered himself an exemplary man of God—*and proud of it.*

3. He felt superior. As a ministry worker, he thanked God that he was *not like other people*. He did not compare himself with God's perfectness but with the imperfectness of his fellow man. As a cleric, he believed he was superior—especially compared to *this tax collector*.

By contrast, the tax collector knew he was needy and asked God for mercy. The Pharisee asked God for nothing.

What can we learn from this passage today?

> **Elitism.** Being one of your church's "tithers" can tempt you (like this Pharisee) to feel superior and judgmental toward "non-tithers."
>
> If you are in ministry, don't let elitism seduce you. You have more time to study the Bible and pray than your fellow Christians, but you are still a sinner saved by grace. Spiritual pride is not attractive.

Conscientiousness. Maybe this Pharisee can teach us something despite his elitism. Giving partners often *forget* to send their promised gifts to mission workers or to their church. The first year I supported a missionary, I gave faithfully every month. Or so I thought. At tax time, I found only eight tax receipts when I should have had twelve. Oops.

Similarly, some giving partners do not increase their giving when they receive unexpected windfalls. Though doing it for the wrong reason, the Pharisee would never have "skipped months" or failed to give a portion of unexpected income.

Off the hook: After giving 10 percent, are tithers "off the hook" for further generosity? Is the other 90 percent under their control to spend as they like? I overheard a believer say casually that after he tithed, he planned to spend his other income to add to his already large classic motorbike collection. Hmmm.

The popular phrase heard in churches almost every Sunday, "God's tithes," leads us to think that God cares only about the ten percent. Haggai 2:8 says, "The silver is Mine, and the gold is Mine, declares the Lord of hosts." One-hundred percent belongs to the Lord. What can we give beyond 10 percent?

The Pharisee, a good tither, saw himself as needed by God. The tax collector saw himself as needing God. A mission leader in the Midwest US often prayed, "Lord, we come to you today as *needy* people—that's the only way we can come."

Prayer: Father in Heaven, I easily see the self-righteousness of this Pharisee, but I find it difficult to see my own. Forgive me for judging others whom I consider less spiritual. I want to be generous, but I focus on the percentage I give rather than on generosity as a lifestyle. And I forget to give when I am busy. Be merciful to me, the sinner. Amen.

BONUS DAY – FINANCIAL PLANNING: THREE QUESTIONS TO GUIDE YOU

> The *foolish* said to the prudent, "Give us some
> of your oil, for our lamps are going out." But
> the prudent answered, "*No,* there will not be
> enough for us and you too; go instead to the
> dealers and buy some for yourselves."
>
> –Matthew 25:8–9

YOU KNOW THE story. Ten virgins planned to attend a wedding. Five wise virgins took extra oil for their lamps, but five foolish virgins "took no oil with them" (Matthew 25:5).

In those days, the groom's wedding party meandered slowly at night to the bride's house. Guests were expected to carry a lamp to honor the newly married couple and bring light to the ceremony. No lamp—no entrance. Wedding crashers existed in Jesus' day too.

When the shout finally came that the bridegroom had arrived, the virgins with no reserve oil asked the prudent virgins to share theirs. But the prudent feared that they too would run out. "Go to the dealers," they said. But while they were buying oil, "the door was shut" (Matthew 25:10).

The point of the parable is to be ready for the Second Coming of Christ. A day is coming when the door will be shut—for eternity.

Can this parable apply to finances also? Yes, especially finances! Underlying this story are three words crucial to financial planning—and to spiritual maturity.

1. ***Assumptions.*** The foolish virgins assumed they knew when the bridegroom would arrive, they assumed they wouldn't need reserves of oil, and they assumed others would bail them out if necessary—last minute scrambling!

But the future does not always behave the way we'd like. For example, do you assume your daughter will receive an all-expenses-paid music scholarship to college? Do you assume that your car has eternal life? Since we mortals have limited control, we must constantly review our assumptions about the future. Assuming you can scramble to safety at the last minute is dangerous for the Second Coming—and in finance.

2. ***Anticipate.*** What events do you anticipate happening over the next few years that will create financial implications? A third child starting school, switching jobs, a parent needing help?

Failure to anticipate is *foolish*—the Greek word is *moros*—moronic! This is strong language from Jesus. Proverbs 22:3 agrees: "The prudent sees the evil and hides himself, but the naïve go on, and are punished for it."

3. ***Boundaries.*** The five wise virgins did not share their oil—they said *no*! They were not acting selfishly. My African friends humorously say they must have been *American* virgins!

Jesus' parable teaches that nothing must be allowed to jeopardize our readiness to meet the Bridegroom at the Second Coming. It is okay to say no.

Jesus himself said no:

- To the Gadarene demoniac who wanted to join the Twelve in the boat

- To His brothers who wanted Him to go immediately to Jerusalem

- To King Herod who demanded Jesus answer him

Jesus had boundaries and so must we. For example, you can say no to:

- Your kids, when they want designer clothes to copy their friends

- Loaning money—give it instead

- Buying stuff on impulse even if you can afford it

Have you seen the humorous sign, usually hanging in auto repair shops: Your failure to plan ahead does not create an automatic emergency for me!

Scottish theologian William Barclay said, "Certain things cannot be obtained at the last minute…"

"When Mary of Orange was dying, her chaplain sought to tell her of the way of salvation. Her answer was, "I have not left this [important] matter to this [late] hour."

Let us not leave salvation to our last hour. Nor financial planning. Ask yourself three questions from the Ten Virgins about your financial future:

- What are your **assumptions**?

- What changes are you **anticipating**?

- What are your **boundaries**?

> **Prayer:** Father in Heaven, You plan ahead. You sent Christ. You even planned me into Your big picture. Help me also to plan—for salvation and in finances. Forgive me when I have irresponsibly tried to "wing it." And help me to set realistic boundaries. Give me the courage to say "no." Amen.

ABOUT THE AUTHOR
www.scottmorton.net

Scott Morton SERVES as International Funding Coach for The Navigators, teaching biblical fundraising and stewardship. In previous assignments, he led Navigator campus and marketplace discipling ministries to students, businesspeople, and missionaries, both stateside and overseas. Then for twelve years, he served as Vice President of The Navigators' US Development Ministry.

Scott enjoys helping people grow in their spiritual journeys through small-group Bible studies and one-on-one mentoring. He is the author of five books, including *Funding Your Ministry*, *Down to Earth Discipling* (NavPress), and *Blindspots* (CMM Press).

He and his wife, Alma, live in Colorado Springs, Colorado, and have two married daughters, a son, and four grandchildren. Scott's hobby is birding.

"I've been raising personal support and coaching ministry workers and leaders around the world since the movies E.T. and Rocky (1 through 4) were hits in America! I've made mistakes—and learned lots of lessons that I'm eager to pass onto you. Browse through the website and find an issue that appeals to you. You'll find others who are on the journey with you, besides me. Learn from them, too! Let's get started!"

— *Scott Morton*

As a pastor or church leader you are asked by parishioners or friends, "God has called me to ministry! But I must raise personal support—what do I do?"

Sadly, many great callings stop right here. But it need not be so. Refer your ministry friends to www.scottmorton.net to empower them with resources for their fundraising ministry. The website includes:

- Up to 100 3-minute videos on felt-need topics like how to ask, who to invite for support, how to minister to donors, how to write newsletters your donors will actually read!

- Blogs and journal entries with helpful lessons learned from American and international gospel workers.

- Downloadable worksheets to help you plan your strategy.

- Bible studies on what the Bible actually says about fundraising.

- A Q and A section.

- A Spanish language tab.

The place to start is with the International Bible Study on Fundraising. Mission-workers around the world say the most helpful part of any fundraising training they receive is the Bible study. Start there.

FUNDING YOUR MINISTRY

HOW MANY POTENTIAL missionaries never reach the field because raising financial support seems too difficult? How many pastors abandon their ministry dreams because of poor pay or fundraising frustration?

It happens too often, but it doesn't have to.

Funding Your Ministry helps ministry workers and pastors break through funding barriers. Do your pastor and missionaries a big favor by introducing them to this book. You can help them

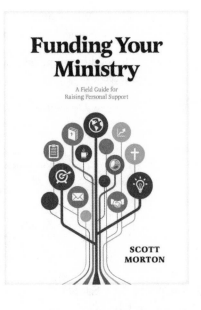

- Discover the biblical path for recruiting and retaining donor support,

- Develop a strategy to reach full support for a lifetime,

- Avoid the common pitfalls of fundraising,

- Learn to manage their money biblically.

Both fundraisers and giving partners will gain valuable insights from Scott Morton as he shares his own funding struggles and victories in raising support. Learn from his experiences and discoveries from the Bible to gain financial freedom to respond to God's call.

In his second year of ministry, Scott Morton was frustrated that his family had to get by on only 60 percent of their budget. His wife gently nudged him, "Are you going to support this family or not?" That caused him to turn to the Bible.

Since discovering for himself the biblical attitudes and skills needed to raise personal support, Morton has helped hundreds of missionaries and ministry leaders in their funding challenges. He has been with The Navigators in student and business discipling ministries, as Upper Midwest Director and Vice President of Development. His current role is International Funding Coach.

> "One of the most practical and needful books that I have ever seen."
>
> *— Dr Howard Fultz, president and founder of Accelerating International Mission Strategies*

> "If you raise support, then *Funding Your Ministry* is a must-read."
>
> *— Ellis Goldstein, Director of Ministry Partner Development, Cru*

DOWN TO EARTH DISCIPLING:

AT LAST, A DISCIPLING GUIDE ANYBODY CAN USE.

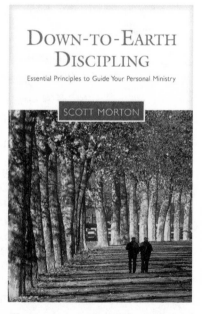

DOWN-TO-EARTH DISCIPLING

Essential Principles to Guide Your Personal Ministry

SCOTT MORTON

WHEN YOU HEAR the "D" word, do you mentally shudder? Thinking about personally discipling others causes believers to take a step back—too scary. Though happily involved in church and Bible studies, it is overwhelming to try to share Christ with friends or family. Or to imagine that we could successfully mentor a new believer. We leave that to the gifted professionals—pastors and mission-workers. But is a professional going to come to your office or to your family gatherings to reach the people in your world? <u>You</u> have a wonderful role to play in advancing the Kingdom!

Here is a personal ministry book for anyone who wants to make even a small difference. It's a practical, friendly, workable guide to everything you need to know about developing your own personal ministry—and it won't terrify you!

"God can use anybody with a willing heart," says author Scott Morton, who describes himself as "not gifted" in discipling. Forged through experience, his realistic approach will inspire you to take the next step in touching friends and family to walk daily with Christ.

So don't be reluctant or worried about discipling. Just be a down-to-earth discipler. God can use you as you are.

> "Scott Morton is an experienced discipler and writes in a reader-friendly fashion. This book will be helpful for both those who just beginning in discipling and for those who are experienced."
>
> — *Jerry Bridges, bestselling author of The Pursuit of Holiness and The Gospel for Real Life*

> "Instead of seeking to have an influence on a large number of people for Christ, we need to give our attention to one person at a time. This is the way the gospel spreads from one person to another—it's as simple as that! Scott has brought us back to the basics in this book, and we need to hear what he is saying."
>
> — *John Stevens, Pastor Emeritus, First Presbyterian Church, Colorado Springs*

BLINDSPOTS

THE BLIND CANNOT LEAD THE BLIND.

(Your pastor needs this book!)

AS A STATE director for The Navigators, I was raising my personal support ministry budget well enough. But I was always short of funding for staff emergencies or ministry expansion opportunities.

Also, my staff and interns were barely getting by. Though they never said a word about it, they struggled to raise enough money to come to regional meetings or to fund family emergencies.

I had unintentionally created an "every staff for himself or herself" mentality. I was so blind, I didn't even help my Regional Assistant who struggled (with tears) in fundraising. "Trust the Lord!" I preached.

I had two blind spots: I thought my staff could figure out their funding without my involvement, and secondly, that I wouldn't need additional money besides my personal budget to lead the ministry. Twice wrong!

— Scott Morton

If you lead a ministry, large or small, in a church or in a mission, in the US or in any country, *Blindspots* is for you. A successful pastor told me, "The topic of money lurks in the back of every pastor's mind. We think about it every day!" But ministry leaders shy away from teaching about money publicly—except when they need it! And that sends out red flags to their constituents.

Blindspots will help you avoid financial and fundraising mistakes in your personal finances, in your staff leadership, and as you lead your entire ministry. It is time to bring a biblical view of money and fundraising into our leadership.